$6⁵⁰ₙ

P9-CQJ-193

THE WAY
Of Traditional Taekwondo

Grand Master Haeng Ung Lee

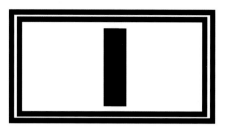

Volume X:

FIRST DEGREE
BLACK BELT - 1단

Copyright © 1995, American Taekwondo Association®
Songahm forms & one-steps are copyright 1983 and later
by the American Taekwondo Association®

This book and Grand Master H. U. Lee's Songahm Taekwondo poome-sae (forms) are covered by copyright law and international copyright conventions. No part or portion may be reproduced without written permission from Grand Master Haeng Ung Lee of the American Taekwondo Association®, World Traditional Taekwondo Union®, and Songahm Taekwondo Federation®.

Written by:

HAENG UNG LEE

Grand Master & Founder
World Traditional Taekwondo Union®
American Taekwondo Association®
Songahm Taekwondo Federation®

Transcribed and Edited by:
Ron Lewis

with information from leading instructors of the Songahm traditional style of Taekwondo.

GRAND MASTER HAENG UNG LEE
Ninth Degree Black Belt
Songahm Taekwondo Founder

종사 이순호

CHIEF MASTER SOON HO LEE
Eighth Degree Black Belt
Executive Vice President

TABLE OF CONTENTS

APPENDIX   *A-1*

GRAND MASTER
HAENG UNG
LEE

SAH-BOO NIM
9th Degree Black Belt

Welcome to the fulfillment of a decision to excel far beyond your expectations. You have crossed the bridge that spans the gap between the novice of Taekwondo and the "expert."

You have reached a plane that few ever achieve. Look back to your training as a white belt student. How many of those students stand proud with you now? How many "made it" and how many quit? You have traveled a long road. You have learned to endure; a precious skill that can be applied to all aspects of life.

THE WAY of Traditional Taekwondo sports a new look at this level to symbolize the new change that you will make. Accepting the rank of Black Belt is no small matter. It is not like promoting from green to purple belt or brown to red. The mystique behind the black belt lends enough burden to one that carries the rank; not to mention the responsibility and expectations.

At this rank, your poome-sae (form) will double in the number of movements; you will take on a new June-bee Jah-sae known as a "half-command position"; the poome-sae (form) will change the way it travels across the Songahm Star pattern; and your do-bok (uniform) will bear new stripes (i.e.; student or trainee stripe) and symbols that will set you apart from others.

Also, you will no longer be referred to as a "student" of Taekwondo, but rather, a "black belt" of Taekwondo.

You are now a cho dan (1st degree) black belt. You have come to a fork in the road and must now choose which path will take you into your future. At this point in your training there are many decisions to make and new goals to create. It is at this point that you begin the "college" of Taekwondo. Up to now, you have trained like a student progressing through school. At the white belt, orange belt, and yellow belt levels, you were in the kindergarten of Taekwondo (only learning basics); at camouflage belt and green belt you covered the elementary years (learning to apply the basics in simple combinations). Purple belt and blue belt levels were like being introduced into Jr. High School with a new level of authority and more advanced application of your gained knowledge. Then, red belt and brown covered your Sr. High School levels as you prepared toward your future in Taekwondo. At the end of this time (as usual in the senior year of school or the summer that follows) you obtained the cho dan (1st degree) recommended black belt. This was a decision making time. Do I go to Taekwondo college and continue my training as a black belt or do I take the skills that I currently have and pursue new goals?

Obviously, you have chosen to go to the "college" of Taekwondo. Here you will choose your career, set your new goals and focus on the next four years that will take you to sahm dan (3rd degree) black belt. During this time, you will gain the knowledge and skills that will develop you into a worthy student of the martial arts. Upon gaining your "bachelor" degree (comparable to the four years of training), you will then strive for the "Master's" degree of yook dan (6th degree)black belt and maybe even your "Doctorate"; becoming Grand Master.

Faced often with frustration and weariness, you were one of the few that beat the odds and excelled beyond others. You reached the first goal. So, do not give up now; don't quit! You have just begun and must press on to a new goal. This "pressing on" will help you be a success in other areas of your life also. Learning to achieve not only goal after goal; but also, goal upon goal... one step at a time.

Use this book to help set your goals and focus on the future ahead. The amount of time you will spend in this one rank alone is often longer than the entire period of time you have trained up to this point.

Realize the importance of starting fresh. Not as a skilled, fully knowledgeable student of the martial arts, but as a beginner in the advanced training of Taekwondo.

Do not fall into the trap of thinking that you have achieved it all. You have accomplished much but there is much more to be learned.

You are not just a black belt, you are a black belt in the most systematic style of martial arts in the world. The instruction, system, and organization of Songahm Taekwondo is "the best the martial arts world has to offer."

Why is Songahm Taekwondo the best of the martial arts as we enter the 21st century? Beyond tradition, Songahm is unique; unlike any other program available. The thee (belt) system, poome-sae (forms) system, teaching system, and children's programs, as well as many other areas, are all examples of how Songahm Taekwondo has surpassed all other martial arts.

Just look at the poome-sae (forms) system itself. Every pattern, from koo geup (9th grade) white belt to koo dan (9th degree) black belt, is connected. One flows into the next (not only in the pattern, but also in the philosophy and tradition). Furthermore, the poome-sae (forms) are more advanced than any other structured poome-sae (forms) system. There are more advanced techniques used at lower levels increasing the skill level of all practitioners and properly reflecting the techniques learned at each level.

> *"I am so proud of this series of Songahm poome-sae (forms). It is a culmination of thousands of years of technique, understanding, philosophy, and tradition. Our poome-sae (forms) must give the best to the students of Taekwondo. If they don't, students won't pursue them. The student wants to know 'why' and 'what will be accomplished.' If a person goes to work each day and works very hard but doesn't have a reason to do so, why would he continue? But, if he knows that it is for his wife, his children, and for the pleasure of a vacation, you can even motivate him to work overtime once in a while. The same is true in Songahm poome-sae (forms). The student can see the immediate and long term rewards and desires to continue."*

Your training can be compared to a beginning artist. First he learns to mix colors .He gains the knowledge of different styles of art and different canvases. He learns about different strokes and differences between types of paints. He knows the technique of drawing a body, face or tree. He has learned the skills necessary to be a great artist. But now, he must apply the technique. He must place the skills he has learned to the surface of a canvas.

The first picture is simple and plain; however, after several attempts, the paintings become more beautiful. His style begins to take shape and his art becomes something unique to him. Many others use the same paint and skills but their paintings come out very different. This is where you are. You have the basics and you understand the different strokes but now you must learn to apply them.

Over the next several years, you will develop a style unique to yourself. It will be the same techniques with the same paints but it will be uniquely you.

Pursue your skills. Take out a new canvas each day and apply your Taekwondo. You will begin to be proud of the graceful yet devastating art that you have learned. This is your time of preparation for becoming a Master of the skill. Now you will develop the qualities of a leader and stretch toward the goal of Master.

THE WAY of Traditional Taekwondo is your art book. Refer to it often and apply the techniques found herein. They will help you develop your skill yet give you the room for your personal touch. Also, refer to lower rank volumes frequently so as to stimulate your memory on lower rank material.

And, on a final note, too many people believe that not attending classes means that you have quit Taekwondo. On the contrary, Taekwondo will be with you always whether you are in a class or not. Besides, the body always needs exercise. Exercise assists in keeping the body healthy and the mind stimulated. If you become too busy, for a time, to attend class, then work out at home a few moments each day. This will keep your mind fresh and your body healthy. Remember that there is no medicine that can take place of good, healthy exercise.

WHAT IS TAEKWONDO TO ME:

Taekwondo was given its name in Korea in 1955, by General Choi, Hong Hi (phonetically = *Chay, Hong Hee*). It was a culmination of the various traditions of ancient fighting skills in Korea and a tangible representation of the human spirit. It is a Korean treasure and considered by most Koreans as a natural resource. In Korea there are three types of Taekwondo.

They are:

PRO-TAEKWONDO -- this type is a full contact sports training that is considered to be entertainment much like professional boxing or wrestling.

SPORT TAEKWONDO -- semi/full-contact training in which the motivation behind the training is competition, trophies, medals, and status. The competitor must be young and excel in Taekwondo talent to be considered for such training. Children, families, and the elderly cannot participate because of the demanding physical requirements. Sport Taekwondo is what has been poorly displayed in several of the past Olympic games.

Sport Taekwondo is divided into weight divisions which actually causes the students to participate in many unhealthy activities, not to mention the encouragement to cheat. When a fighter wants to be in a lower weight division, he/she will starve, devour laxatives, or sit in dry saunas beyond the recommended time to lose the weight. He will do this for several days prior to the actual "weigh-in"; after which, he will eat normal and gain the weight back, therefore appearing to cheat the system by the weight loss. On the other hand, some athletes will drink as much water as possible to gain weight just prior to getting on the scales. It is said that they cannot even bend over without the water running from their mouth because they are so full. And, of course we know how often this kind of pressure to perform leads to drug and steroid abuse.

TRADITIONAL TAEKWONDO -- the "martial art" of Taekwondo. This is an art form that is concerned with the entire person. The person competes with self and is only concerned with personal development. It covers the physical aspects (pro-taekwondo), mental aspects (sports taekwondo), but also adds the emotions as a point of focus, thus giving the Traditional Taekwondo practitioner the most rounded program of the three. Traditional Taekwondo boasts more white collar, elderly, and children practitioners than the other two types; as well as a substantial following among the teen and young adult athletes.

An interesting point about the three types is that a Traditionalist can merge into either of the other two types by just adjusting the physical skills, however it is near impossible for a "pro" or "sports" Taekwondo artist to merge into a traditional training program because of the lack of emotional control, respect, and proper attitude training.

Another important fact is that in both "pro" and "sports" Taekwondo, once you reach a certain age physically, it's over. You are "too old" for the sport. When speaking to many practitioners of the sport (in their late twenties) they often say they are out of shape and too old. You're never too old for Traditional Taekwondo. And, as a matter of fact, the older you get the more you need some form of exercise.

Today's society is in dire need of more "traditional taekwondo" training programs, such as found in Songahm Taekwondo, because of the lack of <u>discipline</u> overwhelming our present and future generations. Traditional Taekwondo teaches mental, physical, and emotional discipline which can result in more success and healthier, happier lives.

Humans and animals both are naturally "lazy." Usually only stimulated to become aggressive when hungry or if their life is threatened. Humans are of a higher intelligence than animals and therefore must gain <u>discipline</u> over these innate, habitual tendencies. Through the evolutionary process, the lack of discipline can create an unhealthy and dying society. Why do people go to work? Because they are hungry or have a drive to survive in this world. Few people would work eight hours a day without the motivation of hunger or survival. Even the rich work as part of the fight to survive at their level of living. Basically, it comes down to the animal instinct of "kill or be killed."

There is a better strategy. Work to produce a better person. Not because you have to, just because you want to. Exercise your body for your health. Now that you have Taekwondo "under your belt," temporary separation from class workouts need not result in a weight gain or muscle loss. Use Taekwondo just a few moments each day (approximately 30 minutes) to keep your body in shape and mind alert. Besides the many benefits you gain from Taekwondo, it is also safer than other cardio-vascular exercises such as aerobics, and safer than other sports like baseball, tennis, and even track.

ABOUT THE WAY:

THE WAY of Traditional Taekwondo is divided into three sections: Reference manuals (such as Vol. A: Philosophy and Traditions), color belt training manuals (white covers), and black belt training manuals (black covers). Each section is then divided into volumes based on rank or subject.

This volume is the first in the series of black belt training manuals. These manuals should be read in order, in their entirety, and not just used to learn a poome-sae (form) or ho-shin-sool (self-defense).

It is suggested that you order your next copy of THE WAY four weeks prior to your next shim-sah (testing) so that you will have it on hand when you receive your new rank. This way, you will have all the answers you need at your fingertips when not in class or a sah-bum nim (Instructor) is not available.

When students advance to the rank of black belt, they tend to engross themselves into the responsibilities of the rank (i.e.; teaching, assisting, duties at Taekwondo school, working for the sah-bum nim [Instructor]) and often train less than they did as a color belt. THE WAY will give you a training guide to help you continue your training even without the assistance of a sah-bum nim (Instructor). A black belt can pick up any volume and still learn about the specifics of individual techniques or they can reference volumes to answer questions students might ask of them that they are not sure about.

Volume X of THE WAY of Traditional Taekwondo was developed for the cho dan (1st degree) black belt student. It covers the seo-gi (stances), chi-gi (strikes), mahk-gi (blocks), and chah-gi (kicks) used at the cho dan (1st degree) black belt level and is not suggested to be a source of self-defense in itself.

Use this and the other manuals as your written guide. Within the pages of this book is almost everything you could ever want to know about the cho dan (1st degree) black belt level of Taekwondo; within your sah-bum nim (Instructor) is the experience and knowledge to help you apply all that is herein written.

HOW TO USE THIS BOOK:

This volume only covers the basic information that should be learned by a cho dan (1st degree) black belt student. For best results, read this manual in the order that it is written. It is important to understand the basics of Taekwondo prior to attempting memorization of the poome-sae (form). Reference should be made to the charts in the appendix section as needed.

Many technical words will be referred to using Korean terminology. In all cases, the English translation will follow in parenthesis; for example, ki-hap (yell). In the Appendix there is a pronunciation key for all the Korean terms used in this manual. Proper nouns, such as the names of poome-sae (forms), will not be followed by an English translation.

As a result of the constant improvements being made by the ranking seniors of Songahm Taekwondo for the advancement of the art, it is possible that some material may change periodically. If information contained in this book conflicts with that which is taught by a Songahm Taekwondo sah-bum nim (Instructor), see the seon-bae sah-bum nim (senior Instructor) in the local do-jahng (Taekwondo facility) for proper guidance.

An important feature in each volume can be found in the Appendix at the back of this book. It is the "Student History" section. In this section, you can record important information about yourself and your training. Each volume has this section so that after many years of training, you will have accurate records of your progress in Songahm Taekwondo.

Dedicated students should read the introductory and philoso-phy chapters of this manual frequently to keep the ideas and understanding of Taekwondo fresh in their minds. Knowing "why" is great motivation in itself to develop the complete student of Taekwondo.

THEME OF THIS VOLUME:

The theme of Volume X, can be seen throughout this entire book. Pictures at the beginning of each chapter display the current Masters of Songahm Taekwondo (as of the most recent printing of this volume).

The rank of "Master" in most styles is an honorary rank and is a title associated with a dan (degree). In Songahm Taekwondo, the title is endowed separate from the rank. A black belt can achieve the rank of yook dan (6th degree) black belt without having earned the title of "Tae-sah Nim (Master Instructor)."

These Masters can be referred to by their English or Korean titles (see the titles in *Volume A: Philosophy and Tradition* or under Chapter VIII of this manual).

An added dimension to the collection of <u>THE WAY of Traditional Taekwondo</u> manuals (that must now be adorning your shelves) would be to set a goal to get the signature of each Master located on these pages. They make special appearances at local, regional, national, and world class events. Who knows, you might even see one as a guest at your next shim-sah (testing).

GUIDANCE FROM THE GRAND MASTER:

I want to truly congratulate you on your most important accomplishment in the art of Taekwondo. You have not just changed thee (belt) colors, you have stepped into a new way of life and a new status among martial artists. You are a "black belt."

Though I have seen thousands upon thousands of students cross over from the position of student to that of black belt, I still feel something special inside myself when I sign the certificate of a new black belt or see the result on a shim-sah (testing) sheet.

Why does this still move me? Because I know the hard work, determination, perseverance, frustration, pain, and glory that is behind achieving the rank. Remember that I too once moved from a color belt to the rank of cho dan (1st degree).

You are now in a new place in your training. You have just topped the peak of your first mountain. Now, however, there is a new, higher mountain to climb. This mountain has steeper paths and more strenuous obstacles, but the rewards are much greater and when you reach the peak, you will not regret a moment. This is the mountain of "mastership."

Along this path you will become a boo sah-bum nim (instructor trainee), a certified sah-bum nim (Instructor), possibly a school owner or a national officer, and eventually a "master." There are no limits to what you can achieve.

Here is an ancient parable I would like to share with you about the green frogs:

"There once was a mother green frog who had many baby green frogs. Everyday, as a mother usually does, she would tell them certain things to do; "do this, do that, go here, go there." But, the little green frogs always seemed to do the opposite. If she said, "sit down," almost inevitably, the little green frogs would stand up.

Contemplating what would happen when she died, she realized that she wanted to be buried on the mountain. So, realizing that to tell the little frogs this would surely be a mistake because they would end up burying her in the valley; she told the little green frogs that when she died, she wanted to be buried on the banks of the river. The little frogs agreed.

Time passed and eventually the mother frog did die. The little green frogs now felt guilty because they never were obedient when she was alive. So, they agreed that they would be true to their mother's last wish and bury her on the banks of the river. Each time that it rains the green frogs become afraid that their mother is going to be washed away by the water. Now, until this day, you can hear the generations of offspring crying on the banks of the rivers in fear of the loss of the mother green frog."

It is so important that we honor our father and mother. We must listen to the wise council of those in authority over us such as our teachers and our Taekwondo sah-bum nim (sah-bum nim [Instructors]). Be true to your sah-bum nim (Instructor). He or she has a lot of wisdom to offer you and can direct and tune your skills. In an age of time when parents must spend their time "making ends meet" there is little time for them to be the disciplinarian and teacher that they should fulfill in the home. Because of this, your Taekwondo sah-bum nim (Instructor) takes on an important role as a substitute "parent." It is their job to help teach you personal discipline, respect, and help point you in the right direction. A black belt does not come with a license to "do as you please" but rather gives you more responsibility to set an example to others in the areas mentioned in the *SONGAHM SPIRIT OF TAEKWONDO.* Do not be deceptive or rebellious or you too may face the same dilemma of the little green frogs.

The root word "sah" in sah-boo nim (grand master) means *teacher* while "boo" means *father.* The word for Instructor, sah-bum nim comes from the same root. Your Instructor is "teacher as a father." Remember that you are setting a goal toward "Mastership." And *Master* in Taekwondo is not "one who rules over slaves" but "one who rules over self." It means that you have learned to control or "master" your body, mind, and emotions.

I encourage you to set your goals high and run toward them at full speed. If you become exhausted in the climb, take a short rest and then start the climb again. You now know that you can achieve your goals, so make your life what you want it to be.

CHIEF MASTER
SOON HO
LEE
JONG-SAH NIM
8th Degree Black Belt

In August of 1984, Grand Master Lee introduced the first in a series of 9 black belt poome-sae (forms). This poome-sae (form) was taught to black belts and sah-bum nim (Instructors) in special clinics and camps and was released in the Taekwondo World Magazine (Vol. 3, No. 4)

The cho dan (1st degree) black belt is compared to a tiger. Like a tiger, he/she has developed physical skills giving him/her the honor of position and status. The cho dan (1st degree) will often become the leader among small groups (clubs or classes within a school) to train toward being a leader of large groups. He/she becomes a leader and must maintain skills and attitude worthy of the role.

As the tiger, the cho dan (1st degree) black belt (unlike the advanced color belts) has learned temperance and is not easily provoked to anger or to an attack. Usually, the tiger/black belt will only resort to physical combat when given no other choice or when he is in need of food. If his stomach is full, he is gentle.

THE TIGER
Cho Dan (1st Degree) Black Belt

Not easily provoked
Has high temperance
Great jumping skill
Leader of small groups

"ShimJun" poetically means to "plant seeds for the future." Just as a mighty pine tree drops seeds into the soil below, so must you, as a black belt, plant seeds for your future.

This can mean planting knowledge into the minds of color belt students, but can also mean planting seeds into your own future (i.e.; career, growth, success, etc.). The great sage once said, "Whatsoever a man sows, that also shall he reap." That simply means, "whatever goes around, comes around." If you plant corn, corn will grow. If you plant kindness and sincerity, that also will grow. If you plant success, that will grow. The problem is too many people quit. And if you plant failure... well, you know what kind of crop is going to spring up.

ShimJun is the "beginner" black belt poome-sae (form). To help understand where you are in your training, consider your training as a Taekwondo student like regular school. As discussed in the introduction, your color belt levels cover your elementary and high school years. When you achieve black belt, you have graduated and now are in "college." However, your first year in college is not often looked at as though you have conquered high school, but rather that you have just begun college; you're a "freshman."

The freshman uses his previous years of knowledge to face this next year. At the freshman level, he builds on his previously learned skills. The cho dan (1st degree) black belt is similar in this regard. The cho dan (1st degree) builds on the skills learned at color belt levels. This is why the poome-sae (form) has few new movements but they are used in a more complex pattern and combination. The cho dan (1st degree) is "fresh" or "new" (a beginner) and should realize his/her place as a new black belt as opposed to a seasoned color belt.

ShimJun (the name of the first black belt poome-sae [form] in the Songahm system) is represented by two squares that connect only at the center point of the Songahm star. Traditionally, ShimJun advances six feet to the east, six feet to the north, then six feet to the west followed by twelve feet to the south (completing the first square and beginning the second). Continuing in the second square travel six feet to the west, then six feet to the north, then twelve feet to the east, and end by returning three feet to the west. When the distance covered is added together, the numerical value of ShimJun is "3" *(6+6+6+12 +6+6+12+3=57, 5+7=12, 1+2=3), a very important number and symbol in Songahm Taekwondo (see Volume A of <u>THE WAY of Traditional Taekwondo</u>).

This numerical system is for the purpose of symbolism, do not use it to create your pattern as each person has a unique measurement based on their stance length).

ShimJun begins like all the color belt poome-sae (forms), facing the east.

As a cho dan (1st degree) black belt, you will begin a new pattern on the Songahm Star. The pattern still utilizes the color belt square but in a different manner. Instead of a rectangle or figure eight pattern that you are familiar with, you will now create two squares in opposite corners of the square (see diagram below).

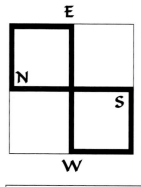

Your path as a black belt takes many new courses now. New challenges and obstacles will teach you even greater perseverance and determination. Do not look at any of these obstacles as too big to overcome. Between you and your sah-bum nim (Instructor), there is no challenge too great. And, remember, when you have succeeded, you gain invaluable experience that will advance you in every aspect of your life.

WHY A BLACK BELT:

"Black" has been the choice of color for this level of rank since the conception of the martial arts. Although many of the other colors have been added or changed, black and white are constants in Taekwondo.

A simple understanding can be found in the following meaning behind the black belt:

> *"The tree has reached maturity and overcome the darkness, it must now begin to plant seeds for the future."*

The student (depicted until now as a tree in growth) has reached a level of maturity. The darkness has passed as a new day of training has arrived. The student must now plant his/her knowledge into the fertile minds of the younger students so that they may grow to be great black belts.

The idea of the black belt can be best understood through an understanding of light and the color spectrum. As explained in Volume III, "light" is the symbol of knowledge. When light hits an object, that object absorbs certain colors and reflects others. For example, if there was a green piece of paper on the ground and the sun's rays struck the paper, the paper would absorb all the colors from the spectrum except green. The green would be reflected into your eyes and you would perceive that the paper was green. Black is unique in the respect that it does not reflect any colors. All the colors of the spectrum are absorbed into the object. If one color escapes, the object is no longer black but appears to be the color that was not retained.

Therefore, the black belt represents that the person wearing the thee (belt) has retained the knowledge (light) of all the lower color belts. If that black belt forgets the skills of green belt, then the green reflects off his/her surface and he/she is perceived to be a green belt level student. But, if he/she retains all the knowledge, then nothing is reflected, all the color is retained, and therefore the thee (belt) is black.

It is very important to understand the tradition behind the color black for a black belt. In Korea, a special ink is used when writing (especially on special documents and artworks). This ink is made from a charcoal stick that is ground down to a fine powder and mixed with water. A special brush is then used to apply the ink to the writing surface. The ink is called "mugk mool" and has come to represent knowledge.

In the Korean culture, a person might refer to someone of vast knowledge as someone whose "head is full of mugk mool"; meaning that he is very knowledgeable. Applying black to your thee (belt) signifies that you have knowledge of Taekwondo (the opposite of white which means "without knowledge").

Think of it as applying the mugk mool (ink) to a piece of white paper. If you continue to apply knowledge (writing) to the paper, it will eventually become black with no white area left uncovered. The paper would then be black. You started as a white belt and have applied knowledge until now; now your thee (belt) is black.

However, if you just think your head is full of "mugk mool" but really you are just trying to dazzle your friends and students with great chah-gi (kicks) and talent, then your head is not full of mugk mool. Rather, you are like a rice stalk that bears no rice. It is tossed in the wind and sways untamed, back and forth. And though it is beautiful to watch as it is pushed back and forth by the wind, it bears no fruit. Its head is empty and it is of no value.

However, the stalk that is full of rice does not sway as easily. Its head is full and the stalk is tame in the wind. The heaviness of the rice (knowledge) causes the stalk to bend forward toward the ground, showing that with knowledge comes humility.

Strive to be one of much mugk mool or one whose stalk is full of rice. Bowing your head as a humble servant of standards, skills, and morals you have been taught as a Songahm black belt. And remember, an empty cart makes the most noise.

Devoting time for the study of the many philosophical meanings and symbols behind the art, its roots and traditions, will give you a better understanding of Taekwondo. Taekwondo is poetically translated as "the art that trains people physically and mentally" (explained in Volume A of <u>THE WAY of Traditional Taekwondo</u>).

Therefore, remember to keep your training balanced. Keep your attitude and ego in check. Train to be excellent, not to show off, but to give others a hero of good morals, great attitude, and excellent technique so that they will have someone for which they can strive to emulate.

SENIOR MASTER
ROBERT
ALLEMIER

BAUP-SAH NIM
7th Degree Black Belt

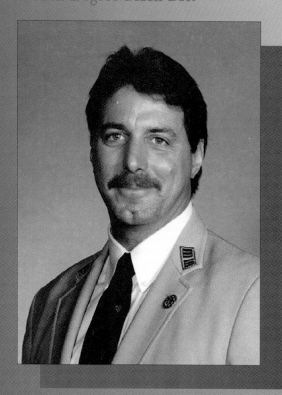

여러가지동작

The black belt level of training brings many new concepts and skills to the arsenal of Taekwondo.

Following are the new movements that must be understood at the black belt level. Perhaps the most significant is the "single arm" movement that replaces the traditional "reaction force" taught to this point. In this chapter, we will cover not only the single arm movement, but also the weon (circular) motion, "advanced" techniques, jong-hahp (compound) movements, advanced retraction, and the use of closed to open hand movement.

NEW TECHNIQUES

"SINGLE ARM" MOVEMENT:

Until now, "reaction force" has been associated with almost every technique that we have covered in your training. Now, all that changes. It's not that we are eliminating reaction force (since it is a law of motion that must take place), we are just changing the way in which it takes place. For the next several levels of rank, "double arm" movement will be rare.

With few exceptions, all techniques will be executed with only one arm in motion. The reaction force is internally rather than externally controlled by the retraction of the opposite arm.

For example: in executing a jee-reu-gi (punch) with the right hand, prior to now we would retract the left hand at the same speed at which the right hand was extending. No longer will the left hand accompany the right. The same jee-reu-gi (punch) at black belt level is a single arm movement. For example: the right and left arms are in a gyeo-roo-gi jah-sae (sparring position). The right arm rapidly strikes the target while the left arm remains in place.

Single arm movement is utilized in most cho dan (1st degree), ee dan (2nd degree), and sahm dan (third degree) techniques. However, sah dan (4th degree) techniques return to "double arm" movement.

Why single arm movement?

Single arm movement is actually the more natural execution of any technique. This is actually the way that techniques are delivered during a sparring match or in actual defensive combat. So, to understand it better, let's evaluate the double arm movement (often referred to as "reaction force").

The double arm movement is taught to new students not because it is more applicable, but because of the new student's lack of coordination, balance, focus of power, and concentration. Observe a white belt and you'll understand the truth in this statement. Over the course of a year or two, the student has learned these necessary skills and can apply them without the help of the retracting arm. That is when the double arm movement is eliminated.

Single arm movement is absolutely necessary in real combat because it is faster, always prepared in any position, and does not telegraph your arsenal.

It's faster because the preparation time is eliminated if the striking tool only needs to travel from its place of rest to the target without waiting for the other arm to gain proper position.

It is prepared in any position because a jee-reu-gi (punch) can travel from the thigh, hip, waist, or gyeo-roo-gi jah-sae (sparring position) to the opponent's target without having to adjust before striking. And, it does not telegraph the arsenal that you carry within your hands and feet. Since you do not have to chamber, the opponent cannot anticipate what technique you are about to use. Why is that important? If you were facing three attackers and one was holding a gun, there was no way of escape, and you feared your life, who would you attack first? The attacker with the gun, of course. You always eliminate your greatest threat first. So, if you telegraphed to an attacker your powerful technique, what area do you think the attacker will be most aware of and try to eliminate first?

The following is an example of the single arm movement.

First, standing in a joo-choom seo-gi (middle stance), extend the left arm forward as if you have executed a right jee-reu-gi (punch).

Next, pull the left arm in rapidly toward the floating ribs. As the left arm nears its resting position, the right arm will begin its execution.

Rapidly extend the right arm to the target.

The single arm movement is primarily designed to leave the opposite arm free for a follow-up technique or for blocking.

Practice this motion using basic techniques until you become comfortable with it. Then, apply it to every striking, thrusting, and blocking technique in your arsenal.

NOTE: *A common misconception is that the retracting arm must be at a complete stop before the opposite arm can begin its movement. Neither is this true or practical. By stopping first, you will decrease the power in the striking arm. However, the striking arm hesitates until the retracting arm is within a couple of inches from its resting position.*

WEON (CIRCULAR) MOTION:

An added dimension to the mahk-gi (blocks) at the black belt level is the weon (circular) motion. This can probably be easily explained by associating it with the famous "wax on - wax off" technique made famous in the "Karate Kid" movie.

The weon (circular) motion is a fluid motion that has no snap or thrust. It "rakes" the oncoming technique out of the way. In most of the weon mahk-gi (circular blocks), the arm rotates around a somewhat stable elbow, causing the hand to travel in a circle.

Why weon (circular) motion?

Besides the grace and beauty often associated with the weon (circular) motions of Taekwondo, weon (circular) motion is very fast and extremely powerful.

When properly evaluated, you will notice that any mahk-gi (block) actually makes a weon (circular) motion. Most mahk-gi (blocks) complete a semicircular motion (however, we don't refer to them as weon [circular] motions).

The full circle motion allows more momentum to be gained in the mahk-gi (block). There are two categories of weon (circular) motion: single hand and double hand. These are then divided into two subcategories: small circles (ex.: circular upset knifehand strike) and large circles (ex.: downwards knifehand strike).

In ShimJun, many of the mahk-gi (blocks) are to be weon (circular) motions. However, practitioners often sacrifice the beauty, art, and correctness of a weon (circular) motion for the "pop" of a do-bok (uniform) when doing a snapping movement. All that the practitioner is doing by this is resorting back

to "beginner" technique and avoiding the advanced movement of black belts.

Grand Master Lee and the power of the circle

*"Following the Mohammad Ali vs. Joe Lewis fight, now only
history, I met with Joe Lewis who was familiar with my
reputation as a traditional Taekwondo Instructor.*

*"Mr. Lewis talked about the innovative twisting of the punch
that Ali had introduced into his boxing styles (then it was not
common to twist your punch). He gloated how the 'twist' was
ineffective based on the fact that he himself had just won the
fight and only straight punched.*

*"I was somewhat perplexed at how he had used one victory
to stifle his ability to learn more about the 'art' of punching.
He had not yet understood the 'power of the circle.'*

*"Concerned that he might leave without the benefit of
learning a lesson through his winning (many winners think
they have nothing more to learn), I proceeded to defend and
explain the power behind the twisting of the hand during a
punch.*

*"After much time passed and I thoroughly explained the
concept to him, he realized the immense power of the circle."*

As most people who follow boxing know, Ali came back and
sported his twisting punch which helped boost him to victory
and the title of "the greatest."

Now, most boxers have incorporated, what martial artists
have long known, the "twisting punch," into their style. What
makes the twisting punch so powerful and why is a twisting
punch being explained in a section on "circular blocks?"

It is because both utilize the power of the circle. As a matter of fact, dol-ah chah-gi (spin kicks) and dol-ah chi-gi (spin strikes) techniques (i.e., spin backfist strike) use this same concept of power enhancement.

When a bullet is shot from a gun, does the bullet travel with or without rotation? It spins even while it is in the barrel of the gun. This allows more momentum to be gained as the bullet slices through the air. This momentum is gained as the bullet completes circle after circle.

The Taekwondo jee-reu-gi (punch) or any other Taekwondo technique, is limited by the fact that a human arm or hand cannot spin invariably. However, the concept can be applied in a limited fashion. For quite some time now you have employed the twisting of the jee-reu-gi (punch) and other techniques. Now, it is time to apply that logic on a grandeur scale...the weon mahk-gi (circular blocks).

The power of the circle is applied here as we allow the hands and arms to travel rapidly in a great weon (circular) motion. The power that is generated at the location of the hands is much greater than the force used to initiate the action. It works much like gears. A large gear moving relatively slow at its center reaches a much greater speed at its outermost point. Think of the way that a ten-speed bike works. Small and large gears are used to give the rider the least amount of effort with the greatest result.

The same is true with a properly applied weon mahk-gi (circular block). A small amount of energy at the shoulder results in a great amount of power at the hands. Thus, applying more power to the axis point multiplies the power at the hands.

Now, it's time to apply this power. Use the photo series on the next page as an example of a weon (circular) motion.

Begin in a right doo-sohn-nahl mahk-gi (double knifehand block). Close your fists and...

...begin to reach upward as you execute a counter-clock-wise rotation of the arms.

The arms continue to move counter-clockwise, using the elbow as an axis, until they are at the head level and just above the shoulders.

Cut the circle slightly and travel diago-nally across the body toward the final position.

And finally, block the oncoming technique with the desired blocking tool.

This motion allows you to gain momentum and move around the oncoming technique without having to chamber all the way to the traditional position.

At the cho dan (1st degree) black belt level, you will use this type of movement while executing the weon doo-ah-rae mahk-gi (circular double low block).

"ADVANCED" TECHNIQUES:

The word "advanced" refers not to a specific technique but to a new way of doing previously learned techniques. Usually the word "advanced" is used to refer to doo-mahk-gi (double blocks). However, the word "advanced" can have two meanings. The advanced application to basic techniques is to develop the black belt further in the areas of coordination, flow, and speed. It is also the fastest way to move from an advanced arm base to a powerful blocking technique.

"Advanced" can mean that a student of a high skill level is executing any technique faster and stronger than that of a beginner. In this explanation however, "advanced" refers to a more difficult execution of particular techniques as described below.

Instead of both arms beginning in parallel positions and moving the same direction, the arms are crossed in opposite positions and move in opposite directions.

An example of how to apply the "advanced" concept to basic techniques can be found on the following page. See your sahbum nim (Instructor) for the proper use of this enhancement on techniques not shown here.

The following is an example of an advanced mahk-gi (block) using the doo-sohn-nahl mahk-gi (double knifehand block) as in Shim-jun Poome-sae.

Begin in a joo-choom seo-gi (middle stance). Prepare the hand as if you just completed the left jee-reu-gi (punch) in Shim-jun Poome-sae, move #21.

As you begin to step into the next position, cross the arms at the chest level with the lead arm (the one that will actually block) on the inside near your face. Both hands are closed.

As you pull the hands in opposite directions, begin to open them.

As you step into a right duweet-goo-bee (back stance), continue pulling the hands in opposite directions until they arrive at the final position of a doo-sohn-nahl mahk-gi (double knifehand block). Be sure to open the hands completely.

WEON (COMPOUND) MOVEMENTS:

Weon (compound) movement refers to a double technique (i.e.; double knifehand low block, double outer-forearm block, square block, etc.) in which the hands are not using the same tool (i.e.; open vs. close) or when two different techniques are executed simultaneously.

For example, a weon doo-ah-rae mahk-gi (compound double low block) would be just like a doo-ah-rae mahk-gi (double low block) with one hand as a fist and the other as a knifehand. Or a jong-hahp ui/ah-rae mahk-gi (compound high/low block) is just like a regular ui/ah-rae mahk-gi (high/low block) with an open and a closed hand combination.

The purpose of weon (compound) movements is to work on a black belt's coordination and concentration. It teaches to control reflexes and to work on memorization. It will also develop the quick reflexes needed in real defense situations against several opponents.

There are several weon (compound) techniques in ShimJun Poome-sae (form).

CLOSED TO OPEN/OPEN TO CLOSED MOVEMENTS:

Until now, techniques always began as they ended. A jee-reu-gi (punch) would chamber with a closed fist and a sohn-nahl chi-gi (knifehand strike) would chamber with an open hand. At the cho dan (1st degree) black belt level, this will rarely be true. Now, the hands will strike in the opposite position (open vs. closed) as they were when they were prepared.

At the color belt levels, concentration is more on the technique, so the shape of the hand is maintained throughout the movement. This gives the student time to concentrate on the more important attributes of the technique.

Now, the black belt must become more fluent, powerful, unpredictable, and fast. In order to achieve this, a reverse concept is incorporated into the black belt's training.

The act of closing or opening a hand during the execution of a technique increases the momentum and speed of the technique, which in turn increases the power (refer to the formula for power: $\mathbf{M}\text{ass} \times \mathbf{V}\text{elocity}^2 = \mathbf{P}\text{ower}$).

A problem occurs in basic technique because the closed-open concept is eliminated and power is decreased.

As a black belt, the reflexes will be trained to automatically choose a technique for attack that is opposite of the natural position of the hand. For example: if you were walking with your hands open to your side and someone attacked you, you should reflexively move your striking tool from the position where it is resting to the target. Since the hand was open, the choice of tools would be a closed technique such as a jee-reu-gi (punch) or deung ju-meok chi-gi (backfist strike). If the hand was closed at rest, then the choice of techniques might be a sohn-nahl chi-gi (knifehand strike) or eop-eun sohn-nahl chi-gi (ridgehand strike).

This will become as instinctive to you as blocking if you apply the concept in your daily training and sparring matches.

RETRACTION:

Another significant movement associated with the black belt is the retraction of technique. Although many techniques remain in place, most chi-gi (strikes) and jee-reu-gi (thrusts) retract immediately upon execution. This is true even in poome-sae (forms).

Think of the execution and rapid retraction like a rubber band that has been stretched to its maximum length. Then, release one end of the band far enough from the surface of your skin (it is probably not a good idea to try this on someone else's body) so that the band snaps your skin and then quickly retracts away from you. If you are successful, you will have felt quite a stinging sensation and probably have a mark by which you can be reminded of this exercise for some time to come.

With this in mind, apply the rapid snap and retraction movement to several basic techniques. Be cautious of joint injuries that can occur from hyperextension of the elbows when practicing this technique without qualified instruction.

Pay close attention when learning ShimJun Poome-sae (form) as this book will explain when to retract a technique and when to leave it extended.

SENIOR MASTER
RICHARD
REED

BAUP-SAH NIM
7th Degree Black Belt

At the cho dan (1st degree) black belt level there are not any new seo-gi (stances). We will however, be looking at the essential role of "walking" as utilized in Songahm Taekwondo.

Though there are no new seo-gi (stances) at this level, it is essential that during the next year of training, you give much attention to all the Taekwondo seo-gi (stances) learned up to this point.

You are a black belt. One part of this position is the responsibility of executing technically correct seo-gi (stances) so that color belt students can use you as a visual example of how they are to do their own techniques.

If you observe the students around you, you could almost tell who was their favorite black belt by the way they did seo-gi (stances) or chah-gi (kicks). This is because when a student is impressed with a certain black belt, he/she begins to subconsciously emulate his/her techniques. Are your seo-gi (stances) worth emulating?

Take the initiative to dedicate time during your training as a cho dan (1st degree) black belt to practice and improve the quality of the seo-gi (stances) you previously learned.

For more details of each seo-gi (stance) you have learned, look in the Volume that corresponds to the level at which the seo-gi (stance) was introduced. A list of the seo-gi (stances) and the volume in which they are explained can be found at the end of this chapter.

GEOD-KEE (WALKING):

This section contains an important aspect of Taekwondo that is often overlooked. That is the movement known as "walking." Few organizations ever recognize the important role that geod-kee (walking) plays in Taekwondo training and combat.

To get from one technique to the next, it is essential to utilize a "step" or "walk." However, few ever discuss this because it seems to come naturally to most people. Or does it? Often, students even question, "How do I get to the next movement?" And in sparring, people often become victims because they "just stood there" and forgot to utilize the important element of geod-kee (walking).

Here is a brief list of types of geod-kee (walking) motions you can utilize in your training:

1.	Walking	...just the way you do it naturally
2.	Double step	...almost like skipping
3.	Hopping	...moving both feet simultaneously
4.	Backing up	...walking backwards (facing target)
5.	Evade (front)	...move the front foot to the left or right
6.	Evade (rear)	...move the back foot to the left or right
7.	Transition	...making a slight walking movement between two positions
8.	Change directions	...steps that change the direction of forward movement
9.	Adjust	...a movement of feet that corrects your path and direction

Why geod-kee (walking)?

All ground animals make use of geod-kee (walking) for travel. Some even swim and walk. Others might swim, walk, and fly. For humans, geod-kee (walking) is a part of the human cycle of life.

An ancient riddle says:

> *"What animal walks on four legs when it's young, two in its prime, and three when it gets old?"*

The answer, of course is man (crawl, walk, and with a cane).

This exemplifies the human cycle of life. When we are born we just lay down; then we begin to crawl; then walk on two legs; then return to laying down at death.

Geod-kee (walking) requires that you "grow up" and gain experience. You must fall many times and must persevere greatly. If humans were to give up as easily when they were learning to walk as they do when they are teens or adults, most would still be crawling in their old age.

Geod-kee (walking) is developed because of a desire to obtain something. A baby's curiosity and desire to grab objects forces them to walk (not to mention mom and dad constantly pushing to see the valued first steps).

Geod-kee (walking) is necessary for exercise. If you don't walk, your body could easily become unhealthy. To increase your health, you increase the speed of your walk (power walking, jogging, and running).

Songahm Taekwondo is different because it emphasizes the geod-kee (walking) more than any other martial art. Most other arts just stand in place or employ short poome-sae (forms).

Many of the martial arts (including Taekwondo) used to not employ poome-sae (form) into their training. However, they later recognized the value of "walking forms" and began to design a series of techniques coupled with geod-kee (walking) to create patterns or poome-sae (named differently in other martial arts).

In poome-sae (forms) we utilize upper body technique to develop the upper body. Although we do chah-gi (kicks) in the poome-sae (forms), the hand foot ratio is very unbalanced. However, when we add the geod-kee (walking) aspect to the poome-sae (forms), we come closer to equalizing the training in the upper and lower body muscles.

Seo-gi (stances) are actually names given to exaggerated geod-kee (walking) steps. This emphasis on bending the knees creates even more exercise in the muscles of the leg, abdomen, and lower back muscles. Just standing or walking normal has minimal benefit (though it is better than becoming a "couch potato").

Geod-kee (walking) is the first Taekwondo technique that any new white belt puts to practice. And, it is the foundation of your kicking techniques. Geod-kee (walking) in itself is its own special "foot technique."

The following is a list of where the description on each seo-gi (form) can be found in <u>THE WAY of Traditional Taekwondo</u>.

VOLUME I -- White Belt
   Mo-ah Seo-gi
      (attention stance)
   Nah-rahn-hee Seo-gi
      (parallel stance)
   Ahp-goo-bee Seo-gi
      (front stance)
   Joo-choom Seo-gi
      (middle stance)

VOLUME II -- Orange Belt
   Duweet-goo-bee Seo-gi
      (back stance)
   Gyeo-roo-gi Seo-gi
      (sparring stance)

VOLUME VIII -- Brown Belt
   Beom Seo-gi
      (rear stance)

SENIOR MASTER KUI B. YOON

BAUP-SAH NIM
7th Degree Black Belt

치기 와 막기

At advanced levels such as cho dan (1st degree) black belt, there are rarely "new" techniques. Usually something new is only something previously learned but now used in a new way or combination. This is true for every "new" mahk-gi (block) you will learn at this level.

There are no new chi-gi (strikes) at the cho dan (1st degree) black belt level. However, use this time of training as an opportunity to perfect striking techniques and develop maximum speed and power with each lower level chi-gi (strike).

AHP KOO-JAH MAHK-GI (FRONT 9-BLOCK):

The koo-jah mahk-gi (9-block) derives its name from the shape it makes when completed. This shape resembles the number "9." It is a traditional technique and has little practical application.

This technique is made up of two mahk-gi (blocks): the ah-rae mahk-gi (low block) and the ahn pahl-mok mahk-gi (inner-forearm block). Both of these mahk-gi (blocks) are used with a slight variation to each.

To learn this technique, it is easier to break it down and practice one arm at a time. Then, after achieving precision in single arm practice, combine the two techniques to complete the koo-jah mahk-gi (9-block).

Preparation: The following example is in a right gyeo-roo-gi seo-gi (sparring stance) with the right hand as the ah-rae mahk-gi (low block) and the left hand as the ahn pahl-mok mahk-gi (inner-forearm block).

Chamber the hands as if you were prepared to do a ui/ah-rae mahk-gi (high/low block) to the front with the right hand in the high position.

Next, pull the left arm upward toward the solar-plexus (traveling outside of the opposite arm) while pushing the right arm downward toward a ah-rae mahk-gi (low block) position.

Finally, complete this technique by stopping the left arm across the chest with the palm facing in toward the body; and, the right arm stops with the hand centered on the body just below the groin level. Notice the nine shape made by the positions of the arms (a reversed 9 in this photo).

There are actually three types of koo-jah mahk-gi (9-blocks). They are used differently at different levels of training.

The three renditions are:

Koo-jah mahk-gi (9-block) -- used from a joo-choom seo-gi (middle stance) and centered on the body.

Ahp koo-jah mahk-gi (front 9-block) -- usually in a deweet-goo-bee (back), gyeo-reu-gi (sparring), or beom seo-gi (rear stance) and positioned over the leading leg. Used in ShimJun.

Ui koo-jah mahk-gi (High 9-block) -- used in the ee dan poome-sae, JungYul. The rear hand takes a ui mahk-gi (high block) position over the head as opposed to across the chest.

WEON DOO-SOHN-NAHL AH-RAE MAHK-GI (CIRCULAR DOUBLE KNIFEHAND LOW BLOCK):

The weon doo-sohn-nahl ah-rae mahk-gi (circular double knifehand low block) ends in the same position as the doo-sohn-nahl ah-rae mahk-gi (double knifehand low block), however, the execution of this technique varies dramatically.

This motion is to be a long and graceful movement. Be sure to keep the arms extended throughout the first 3/4 of the movement.

Follow the description on the next page to learn the basics of executing a weon (circular) motion and you can apply it to different types of techniques.

Preparation: The following example is in a left duweet-goo-bee seo-gi (back stance) with the arms in a doo-sohn-nahl mahk-gi (double knifehand block).

Begin in a right doo-sohn-nahl mahk-gi (double knifehand block).

As you begin your motion, close your hands and begin to reach upward traveling in a counterclockwise motion.

The arms continue to move counterclockwise, using the elbow as an axis, until they are level with the head and just above the shoulders.

Cut the circle slightly and travel diagonally across the body toward the final position.

And finally, block the oncoming technique with the knife edge of the right hand.

JONG-HAHP DOO-AH-RAE MAHK-GI (COMPOUND DOUBLE LOW BLOCK):

The jong-hahp doo-ah-rae mahk-gi (compound double low block) is the same technique as the doo-sohn-nahl ah-rae mahk-gi (double knifehand low block) with the exception that the rear hand is in a fist rather than a knifehand.

Preparation: The following example is in a right duweet-goo-bee seo-gi (back stance), as if placing the foot down from the

left dol-ryeo chah-gi (round kick) in move #53 of ShimJun Poome-sae.

Prepare the hands behind the body and bent to 90 degree angles as seen in the photo to the left. Both hands are closed.

Drive the hands downward, across the body, as the left hand begins to open.

Both hands execute this technique as normal for a doo-ah-rae m a h k - g i (double low block) or doo-

sohn-nahl ah-rae mahk-gi (double knifehand low block). The only exception is that the final position of the hands is with the front hand open and the rear hand closed.

JONG-HAHP SAH-GAHK MAHK-GI (COMPOUND SQUARE BLOCK):

The jong-hahp sah-gahk mahk-gi (compound square block) is executed exactly as a regular sah-gahk mahk-gi (square block) except that the bah-kaht pahl-mok mahk-gi (outer-forearm block) is changed to an bah-kaht sohn-nahl mahk-gi (outer-knifehand block). The fist of the ui mahk-gi (high block) is closed.

Preparation: Stand in a right duweet-goo-bee seo-gi (back stance) as in move #54 of ShimJun Poome-sae.

From this position, you will make a 270 degree (3/4 of a circle) turn in a counterclockwise rotation.

As you begin to turn, place the right hand on the floating ribs (fist with palm up) as if to chamber for a ui mahk-gi (high block). Place the left arm across the solar-plexus, chambering for a bah-kaht pahl-mok mahk-gi (outer-forearm block) (fist palm up).

Next, move both arms simultaneously, allowing the right hand to follow the lapel of the do-bok (uniform) upwards and the left hand to travel the same as a regular bah-kaht pahl-mok mahk-gi (outer-forearm block).

Note: the hands will travel only inches from each other until they have reached a position approximately in front of the nose, at which point they will break apart and continue toward their target. The left hand will begin to open immediately upon executing the technique.

Finally, complete this technique by letting the right arm end in a ui mahk-gi (high block) approximately three inches from the forehead and at a 45 degree angle; and, allowing the left arm to end in an bah-kaht sohn-nahl mahk-gi (outer-knifehand block) in front of the face, just below eye level.

AHN JOHK PAHL-MOK MAHK-GI (INWARD INNER-FOREARM BLOCK):

The ahn-johk pahl-mok mahk-gi (inward inner-forearm block) is one of the more difficult techniques in which to develop power. However, it is used in conflicts without the practitioner even realizing that he/she has used this technique.

The inner-forearm is the blocking tool and this technique is usually used to deflect yeop chah-gi (side kicks). The path on which it travels is very short and it is absolutely necessary to use the twisting of the hips for increased power.

Preparation: Begin in a right ahp-goo-bee seo-gi (front stance) executing a left bah-tahng sohn mahk-gi (palm block) *as in move #38 of ShimJun Poome-sae.*

As you move the right leg inward to a goob-eun mo-ah seo-gi (low closed stance). Next, extend the right hand downward toward the your backside until the arm is almost straight (the palm of the hand is twisted slightly out toward the opponent).

Pull the arm rapidly inward with the hand raking across the thigh area. The hand twists counterclockwise approximately 160 degrees so that the oncoming technique is blocked with the inner-forearm portion of the lower arm.

Complete this technique with the hand stopping adjacent to the thigh.

SOHN-NAHL UI/AH-RAE MAHK-GI (HIGH/LOW KNIFEHAND BLOCK):

This technique is identical to the regular ui/ah-rae mahk-gi (high/low block) with the exception that the hands are open.

This is a "traditional" technique and is not meant for practical application. However, much time needs to be given to the perfecting of this skill as it develops necessary gross motor skills, and of course, you will be judged on this technique in poome-sae (forms) competition and shim-sah (testing).

This mahk-gi (block) is as if someone is striking you with a jee-reu-gi (punch) (to face) and a ahp chah-gi (front kick) (to groin) at the same time. However, remember that this technique is not for practical use. The proper tool is the knife edge of the hand.

Preparation: Stand in a joo-choom seo-gi (middle stance) with a right sohn-nahl chi-gi (knifehand strike) as if you just completed move #62 of ShimJun Poome-sae.

NOTE: Remember to close the hands just prior to chambering for this technique.

As you begin the 180 degree counter clockwise rotation, begin to chamber with the right hand up as if it had just completed an ahn pahl-mok mahk-gi (inner-forearm block) and the left hand down as if it had just completed a ah-rae mahk-gi (low block).

As you step into a mo-ah seo-gi (closed stance), in a simultaneous motion, rotate the right arm (using the elbow as a pivot point) in a counterclockwise motion, passing inside the left arm; and, rotate the left arm (using the elbow as a pivot point) in a counterclockwise motion, passing outside the right. Both hands immediately begin to open as the technique is executed.

Continue this motion until the right arm has ended in a right sohn-nahl ah-rae mahk-gi (knifehand low block) and the left arm has ended in a left sohn-nahl mahk-gi (knifehand block).

To develop more power, use the twisting of the hips to pull the techniques into place. Both of these techniques are now "swinging" techniques.

SENIOR MASTER
IN HO
LEE
BAUP-SAH NIM
7th Degree Black Belt

The layman often considers a black belt "good" or "not so good" based on his/her ability to chah-gi (kick) with flexibility or power.

Although we know that the best black belt is one that is skilled in every area, the general public wants to see the awesome Taekwondo "kicks."

At this level, the only new chah-gi (kicks) in the poome-sae (form) are the jee keo (foot stomp) and the mee-reo yeop chah-gi (pressing side kick).

JEE KEO (FOOT STOMP):

The jee keo (foot stomp) is a technique designed to strike the instep or shin of an attacker or to strike a downed attacker (closest target). It is very powerful because the weight of the entire body is over the foot.

When executing a jee keo (foot stomp), drive the heel of the foot into the target. If an attempt to scrape the shin is desired, the knife edge of a pair of hard sole shoes may be the prime striking tool.

This technique is a thrusting motion as the knee pushes it to the target.

Preparation: Stand in a left duweet-goo-bee seo-gi (back stance) having just executed move #23 of ShimJun Poome-sae.

Lift the left foot upward as high as possible (but not like an ahp ol-reo chah-gi [stretch kick]) toward the front. Allow the foot to point upward and keep the knee slightly bent.

Complete the stomp by striking the target with the heel of the foot.

Avoid "slapping" the ground with the whole foot. Focus all the power into the heel or foot-sword when you execute this technique.

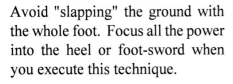

MEE-REO YEOP CHAH-GI (PRESSING SIDE KICK):

This technique is identical to the regular yeop chah-gi (side kick) with the exception that it is executed downward, usually as a mahk-gi (block) against a ahp chah-gi (front kick) or as an attack toward the knee, shin or a downed attacker.

In ShimJun, the mee-reo yeop chah-gi (pressing side kick) is executed as a tension movement (3-5 seconds).

Preparation: Stand in a left duweet-goo-bee seo-gi (back stance) as if just having completed move #70 (jee-reu-gi [punch]) of ShimJun Poome-sae.

As the left foot slightly pivots away from the target, lift the right knee to a comfortable position. The leg should be angled toward the opponent's target. With tension, press the heel downward toward the target.

Complete the technique by pressing to full extension.

SENIOR MASTER
BILL
CLARK

BAUP-SAH NIM
7th Degree Black Belt

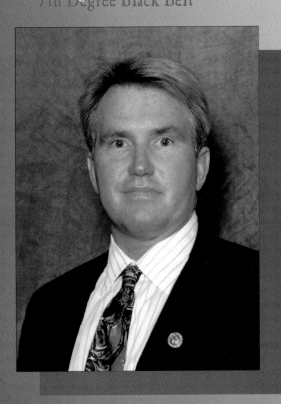

ShimJun is the first of the black belt poome-sae (forms) in the Songahm system. You might have noticed that it is not numbered like all the previous poome-sae (forms) (i.e.; Songahm **Il-jahng**)

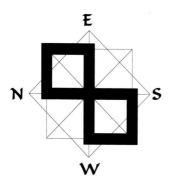

ShimJun takes its place on the color belt star but in a position unlike any previous poome-sae (form). In this diagram, you'll notice that it is two small squares situated on opposite sides of the color belt square. One is in the NE corner and the other in the SW corner.

This poome-sae (form) is set up similar to InWha Il-jahng with the idea that the opposite side of each square repeats itself (with the opposite hand and foot). The corners of each square, however, are not consistent with the opposite. This is to challenge the student in both memory and concentration.

Each poome-sae (form) must have a new challenge, just as life itself has new challenges each day. It is

The following squares on the bottom right corner of the pages in this chapter make up an animated mini-movie showing the path that a student takes on the Songahm Star when executing ShimJun Poome-sae. To see the effect of this mini movie, hold the book firmly and place your thumb on the bottom right corner of this page. Focus your eyes on the square and then rapidly flip through the pages. You will see each frame rapidly display the progress of ShimJun.

through and by these obstacles that we are able to improve ourselves and our lives.

In the Songahm system, the poome-sae (forms) have been arranged, not only to help a student develop both sides of the body and technique equally, but also for easy memorization.

All of the poome-sae (forms) connect from white belt to koo dan (ninth degree) black belt. This is because if there is not a complete path, you cannot reach your final destination. Often poome-sae (forms) do not connect and are tangled, showing no real structure. By having each poome-sae (form) connect, we can see how each level is a crucial link in the entire Songahm structure. Just as in the chain of command, most often found in military surroundings or in your do-jahng (Taekwondo facility), you can see there are lower and higher levels. And, to get from one level to the other you must first go through the middle levels.

This connection could be looked at like a map of your country. There are many roads, highways, and interstates. These are placed there so you can get from one destination to the next. Without them, you could still reach the destination, but it would take much longer and add more "wear and tear" on your body and mind.

Throughout history, man has improved upon the idea of this connection by inventing ways to speed up the travel time between points "A" and "B." First were paths, then dirt roads, then paved roads, then highways, then freeways and interstates. Now, we even have planes to decrease the travel time. But remember, planes are in the clouds and you can never actually reach your destination with your head in the clouds. You have to come down first and use another mode of transportation.

Songahm has done for Taekwondo what the transportation

system did for the world. Now, students can reach the same destination as before but with more efficiency, less wear and tear, and in less time. This is due to the innovative structure of the Songahm system.

The Songahm system was designed as a "curriculum" to bring a student from white belt to black belt and beyond. Poome-sae (forms) are the textbook of that curriculum.

In most martial arts, there is little or no idea of a curriculum. Many times, the sah-bum nim (instructor) has taught the student all he/she knows before the student reaches black belt. Then, without anything new to learn, the student becomes bored and quits.

In Songahm Taekwondo, the curriculum was carefully laid out to included everything a student would ever need to learn and then the program was spread out over all the ranks in the system. This gave new and exciting material at each level and

SYMBOL OF INFINITY

insured that a student would not miss any important training throughout his/her complete Taekwondo career. This not only takes a student to black belt, but beyond black belt and into Taekwondo infinity.

The diagram of Shim-jun Poome-sae is the symbol of infinity (see diagram to the right). The con- cept behind the symbol of infinity is "eternal, never ending." This is representative of the black belt's perseverance. Also, just as the universe extends outward to infinity with vast amounts of resources and knowledge hidden from us by darkness and distance, so too are the levels of Master. Those ranks are full of knowledge and resources that the average student and sah-bum nim (instructor) do not see. It is as if we viewed these ranks through a dark glass. Only when we have achieved that which is necessary will we begin to look through the glass clearly and see to the ends of infinity.

Poome-sae means "THE WAY" or pattern (DO). Your pattern in life determines if you are happy or miserable. If your pattern is sloppy with crooked lines, then that is a reflection of having no desire, focus or direction; usually ending in an unfulfilled life. But, if your pattern is clean with straight lines, this is a reflection of a desire to accomplish your goals, giving it your best, and knowing your direction. This will result in a fulfilled and prosperous life. This is true in Songahm Poome-sae, your Taekwondo pattern, which is the culmination of the "orthodox" of Taekwondo.

The purpose is to eventually, one poome-sae (form) at a time, form a circle, the "Songahm circle (formed by connecting all nine points of the Songahm Star)." It gradually changes, by adding new poome-sae (forms) and techniques, until it is perfected. Each line becomes another step toward completion, each poome-sae (form), another phase. Each day from white belt, to black belt, to Master is the connection of that circle. At Master you have completed and perfected the circle. *(See chapter VI in Volume A for further details.)*

Why a circle? Because it represents perfection. If you had to choose a rock from a mound of rocks, and there was one that was smooth and round, most would choose that one because it is close to our perception of perfect. Why? Because people look for perfection in nature which is actually the reflection of the perfection they would like to see in themselves.

Consider the things we associate in nature with our own lives. A straight stick represents a straight path. A clear diamond is like a clear mind. Consider also the things we find beautiful. Diamonds, gems, gold and silver. We see things in gold that we would like to be. Gold never changes its color, it is true and loyal to the color. It is shiny and beautiful, and if pure, will remain so. Gem stones, as with mountains change little over thousands of year. People have a desire to be more beautiful and live longer, so therefore we are attracted to these qualities.

ShimJun is designed to challenge the black belt. So often color belt students ask why you have to remain in rank for over a year...ShimJun is one of the reasons.

The time in rank is not just for learning your poome-sae (form), it is to give you the necessary experience in rank before advancing you to a new level. Experience is the best teacher you have at the black belt level.

NEW TECHNIQUES in SHIMJUN POOME-SAE

SEO-GI (stances)
(no new seo-gi)

CHI-GI & MAHK-GI (strikes & blocks)

Mahk-gi (block)
Koo-jah mahk-gi (9-block)
Jong-hahp doo-sohn-nahl mahk-gi (compound double knifehand block)
Jong-hahp doo-ah-rae mahk-gi (compound double low block)
Jong-hahp sah-gahk mahk-gi (compound square block)
Ahn Johk pahl-mok mahk-gi (inward inner-forearm block)
Ui/ah-rae sohn-nahl mahk-gi (high/low knifehand block)

CHAH-GI (kicks)
Jee keo (foot stomp)
Mee-reo Yeop Chah-gi (pressing side kick)

SHIMJUN POOME-SAE

Side	Technique	Seo-gi (stance)	Target
1. L	Double Inner-forearm Block *Doo-ahn Pahl-mok Mahk-gi*	Middle *Joo-choom*	H
2. R	Upset Punch *Jae-chyeo Jee-reu-gi*	Middle *Joo-choom*	H
⑤ 3. L	Upset Palm Block *Jae-chyeo Bah-tahng Sohn Mahk-gi*	Middle *Joo-choom*	M
4. R	Punch *Jee-reu-gi*	Middle *Joo-choom*	M
5. L	Punch *Jee-reu-gi*	Middle *Joo-choom*	M
6. L	Adv. Double Knifehand Block *Adv. Doo-sohn-nahl Mahk-gi*	Back *Duweet-goo-bee*	H
② 7. L	Circular Double Knifehand Block *Weon Doo-sohn-nahl Mahk-gi*	Back *Duweet-goo-bee*	Lw
8. R	Stomp Kick *Jee Keo*	Middle *Joo-choom*	
9. R	Backfist Strike *Deung Ju-meok Chi-gi*	Middle *Joo-choom*	H
10. R	#3 Side Kick *Yeop Chah-gi Sahm-beon*		M/H
⑥ 11. R	High/Low Block *Ui/Ah-rae Mahk-gi*	Closed *Mo-ah*	H/Lw
12. L	High/Low Block *Ui/Ah-rae Mahk-gi*	Closed *Mo-ah*	H/Lw
13. R	Knifehand Low Block (tension) *Sohn-nahl Ah-rae Mahk-gi*	Rear *Beom*	Lw
14. R	Front Kick *Ahp Chah-gi*		M/H
③ 15. R	#3 Jump Hook Kick *Ddee-eo Nahk-ah Chah-gi Sahm-beon*		H
16. R	9-block *Ahp Koo-jah Mahk-gi*	Sparring *Gyeo-roo-gi*	Lw/M
17. R	Double Inner-forearm Block *Doo-ahn Pahl-mok Mahk-gi Joo-choom*	Middle	M
18. L	Upset Punch *Jae-chyeo Jee-reu-gi*	Middle *Joo-choom*	H

(5)

19. R	Upset Palm Block	Middle	M
	Jae-chyeo Bah-tahng Sohn Mahk-gi	*Joo-choom*	
20. L	Punch	Middle	M
	Jee-reu-gi	*Joo-choom*	
21. R	Punch	Middle	M
	Jee-reu-gi	*Joo-choom*	

(2)

22. R	Adv. Double Knifehand Block	Back	
	Adv. Doo-sohn-nahl Mahk-gi	*Duweet-goo-bee*	
23. R	Circular Double Knifehand Block	Back	Lw
	Weon Doo-sohn-nahl Mahk-gi	*Duweet-goo-bee*	

(7)

24. L	Stomp Kick	Middle	
	Jee Keo	*Joo-choom*	
25. L	Backfist Strike	Middle	H
	Deung Ju-meok Chi-gi	*Joo-choom*	
26. L	#3 Side Kick		M/H
	Yeop Chah-gi Sahm-beon		
27. L	X-block	Low Closed	Lw
	Eot-geol Mahk-gi	*Goob-eun Mo-ah*	
28. L	Head grab	Low Closed	H
	Mok-teol-mee Jahp-kee	*Goob-eun Mo-ah*	
29. R	Knee Strike		Lw
	Moo-reup Chi-gi		
30. L	Knifehand Low Block (tension)	Rear	Lw
	Sohn-nahl Ah-rae Mahk-gi (T)	*Beom*	

(3)

31. L	#1 Front Kick		M/H
	Ahp Chah-gi Il-beon		
32. L	#3 Jump Hook Kick		M/H
	Ddee-eo Nahk-ah Chah-gi Sahm-beon		
33. L	9-block	Sparring	M/Lw
	Ahp Koo-jah Mahk-gi	*Gyeo-roo-gi*	

(3)

34. R	Compound Square Block	Back	M/H
	Johg-hahp Sah-gahk Mahk-gi	*Duweet-goo-bee*	
35. R	Upset Knifehand Strike	Back	M
	Jae-chyeo Sohn-nahl Chi-gi	*Duweet-goo-bee*	
36. L	Reverse Vertical Punch	Front	M
	Bahn-dae Sae-woon Jee-reu-gi	*Ahp-goo-bee*	

ABBREVIATION KEY

| L-left | R-right | | H-high | M-middle | Lw-low |
| SP-solar plexus | RI-ribs | CH-chin | PH-philtrum | TP-temple |

37. R	**#3 Jump Front Kick** *Ddee-eo Ahp Chah-gi Sahm-beon*		M/H
38. L	**Reverse Palm Strike** *Bahn-dae Bah-tahng Sohn Chi-gi*	Front *Ahp-goo-bee*	H
⑤ **39. R**	**Inward Inner-forearm Block** *Ahn Johk Pahl-Mok Mahk-gi*	Low Closed *Goob-eun Mo-ah*	Lw
40. L	**Horizontal Elbow Strike** *Soo-pyeong Pahl-goop Chi-gi*	Middle *Joo-choom*	M
41. L	**Knifehand Strike** *Sohn-nahl Chi-gi*	Middle *Joo-choom*	H

42. L	**Knifehand X-block** *Sohn-nahl Eot-geol Mahk-gi*	Low Closed *Goob-eun Mo-ah*	H
43. L	**Knifehand Strike** *Sohn-nahl Chi-gi*	Low Closed *Goob-eun Mo-ah*	H
⑤ **44. L**	**Knee Strike** *Moo-reup Chi-gi*		
45. R	**Ridgehand Block (tension)** *Eop-eun Sohn-nahl Mahk-gi*	Rear *Beom*	H
46. R	**Fingertip Thrust (slow)** *Sae-woon Sohn-geut Jee-reu-gi (S)*	Rear *Beom*	H

47. R	**Spin Hook Kick** *Dol-ah Nahk-ah Chah-gi*		M/H
48. L	**Low Block** *Ah-rae Mahk-gi*	Middle *Joo-choom*	Lw
④ **49. L**	**Inner-forearm Block** *Ahn Pahl-mok Mahk-gi*	Middle *Joo-choom*	H
50. L	**Punch** *Jee-reu-gi*	Middle *Joo-choom*	M

51. L	**#3 Side Kick (slow)** *Mee-reo Yeop Chah-gi Sahm-beon*		
52. L	**Round Kick** *Dol-ryeo Chah-gi*		M
④ **53. L**	**Round Kick** *Dol-ryeo Chah-gi*		M/H
54. L	**Compound Low Block** *Johg-hahp Ah-rae Mahk-gi*	Sparring *Gyeo-roo-gi*	Lw

55. L	**Compound Square Block** *Johg-hahp Sah-gahk Mahk-gi*	Back *Duweet-goo-bee*	M/H
③ **56. L**	**Upset Knifehand Strike** *Jae-chyeo Sohn-nahl Chi-gi*	Back *Duweet-goo-bee*	M
57. R	**Reverse Vertical Punch** *Bahn-dae Sae-woon Jee-reu-gi*	Front *Front stance*	M

58. L	#3 Jump Front Kick			M/H
	Ddee-eo Ahp Chah-gi Sahm-beon			
59. R	Reverse palm strike		Front	H
	Bahn-dae Bah-tahng Sohn Chi-gi		*Ahp-goo-bee*	
⑤ 60. L	Inward Inner-forearm Block		Low Closed	Lw
	Ahn Joke Pahl-mok Mahk-gi		*Goob-eun Mo-ah*	
61. R	Horizontal Elbow Strike		Middle	M
	Soo-pyeong Pahl-goop Chi-gi		*Joo-choom*	
62. R	Knifehand Strike		Middle	H
	Sohn-nahl Chi-gi		*Joo-choom*	

63. L	High/low Knifehand Block		Low Closed	H/Lw
	Ui/Ah-rae Sohn-nahl Mahk-gi		*Goob-eun Mo-ah*	
64. R	High/low Knifehand Block		Low Closed	H/Lw
④	*Ui/Ah-rae Sohn-nahl Mahk-gi*		*Goob-eun Mo-ah*	
65. L	Ridgehand Block (tension)		Rear	H
	Eop-eun Sohn-nahl Mahk-gi (T)		*Beom*	
66. L	Fingertip Thrust (slow)		Rear	H
	Sae-woon Sohn-geut Jee-reu-gi (S)		*Beom*	

67. L	Spin Hook Kick			M/H
	Dol-ah Nahk-ah Chah-gi			
68. R	Low Block		Middle	Lw
④	*Ah-rae Mahk-gi*		*Joo-choom*	
69. R	Inner-forearm Block		Middle	H
	Ahn Pahl-mok Mahk-gi		*Joo-choom*	
70. R	Punch		Middle	M
	Jee-reu-gi		*Joo-choom*	

71. R	#3 Side kick (slow)			
	Yeop Chah-gi Sahm-beon (slow)			
72. R	Round Kick			M
④	*Dol-ryeo Chah-gi*			
73. R	Round Kick			M/H
	Dol-ryeo Chah-gi			
74. R	Compound Low Block		Sparring	Lw
	Johg-hahp Ah-rae Mahk-gi		*Gyeo-roo-gi*	

ABBREVIATION KEY

L-left	R-right		H-high	M-middle	Lw-low
SP-solar plexus	RI-ribs	CH-chin	PH-philtrum	TP-temple	

┌ 75. R #2 Jump Side Kick   M/H
│   *(Step) Ddee-eo Yeop Chah-gi Ee-beon*
│ 76. R Adv. Double Outer-forearm Block Back   H
④   *Adv. Doo-bah-kaht Pahl-mok Mahk-gi   Duweet-goo-bee*
│ 77. L Reverse Punch   Back   M
│   *Bahn-dae Jee-reu-gi   Duweet-goo-bee*
└ 78. L Circular Dbl. Outer-forearm Block Back   Lw
              Weon Doo-bah-kaht Pahl-mok Mahk-gi   Duweet-goo-bee

┌ 79. L Adv. Double Outer-forearm Block Back   H
│   *Adv. Doo-bah-kaht Pahl-mok Mahk-gi   Duweet-goo-bee*
③ 80. R Reverse Punch   Back   M
│   *Bahn-dae Jee-reu-gi   Duweet-goo-bee*
└ 81. R Circular Dbl. Outer-forearm Block Back   Lw
              Weon Doo-bah-kaht Pahl-mok Mahk-gi   Duweet-goo-bee

*On the previous pages, the spaces between the lines (set off by brackets) separates
segments of techniques. The number in the circle represents the number of movements in that segment. The reverse (white number in black box) numbered
techniques (#21, #41, & #61) designate the techniques on which a ki-hap (yell) is
executed. This poome-sae (form) has 81 movements and should take approximately
2:05 to 2:10 (min:sec) to complete from the first "chah-reot (attention)," before
bowing, to the final "shi-uh (at ease)."*

N = No retraction   **R** = immediate **R**etraction
S = Single arm movement   **D** = Double arm movement
T = Tension   **M** = slow-**M**otion

The poome-sae (form) "key" (as seen above) is located on each of the
following pages. It is found horizontally across the pages between the two
photographs for easy reference. The following is a brief description of
each abbreviation.

N - No retraction   This means that you do not retract the technique
                                   immediately upon its execution.

R - immediate Retraction   This means that you retract the technique imme-
                                   diately upon execution.

S - Single arm movement   Do not use full reaction force when executing
                                   this technique (see Chapter II - Types of Move-
                                   ment)

D - Double arm movement   Use full reaction force when executing this
                                   technique.

T - Tension   Slowly execute this technique for a count of five
                                   seconds

M - slow-Motion   Slowly execute this technique for a count of two
                                   seconds

SHI-UH JAH-SAE
(At Ease Position)

Begin from the SHI-UH JAH-SAE (at ease position). This is similar to the "at ease" position used in the military. Relax in this position until the next command is given.

N = No retraction   R = immediate **Retraction** / S = Single arm movement   D = Double arm movement / T = Tension   M = slow-Motion

CHAH-REOT
(Attention)

At the command, "chah-reot (attention)," the student will come to attention, lightly slapping the thighs with the hands and feet in a MO-AH SEO-GI (attention stance).

KYEONG-NEH
(Bow)

Bow to approximately a 45 degree angle toward the east (or in the direction that you will begin to execute this poome-sae [form]).

Note that in the insert to the left, the back is curved as Chief Master Lee bows.

N = No retraction   R = immediate **Retraction** / S = Single arm movement   D = Double arm movement / T = Tension   M = slow-Motion

BAHN JEE-DO-JAH JAH-SAE
(Half-command Position)

Move the left foot outward (shoulder width) to a nah-rahn-hee seo-gi (parallel stance). Place the right fist adjacent to the floating ribs with the left arm across the chest and the left fist adjacent to the right collarbone.

Take this position on the command, "JUNE-BEE."

1. Left foot steps toward the east to a JOO-CHOOM SEO-GI (middle stance), pivoting on right heel with left toe and right heel on east-west line. Execute a LEFT DOO-AHN PAHL-MOK MAHK-GI (double inner-forearm block). [D,N]

N = **N**o retraction   **R** = immediate **Retraction** / **S** = **S**ingle arm movement   **D** = **D**ouble arm movement / **T** = **T**ension   **M** = slow-**M**otion

2. Without stepping, execute a RIGHT JAE-CHYEO JEE-REU-GI (upset punch) to the high section. [S,R]

3. Without stepping, execute a LEFT JAE-CHYEO BAH-TAHNG SOHN MAHK-GI (upset palm block). [S,N]

N = No retraction   R = immediate **Retraction** / S = Single arm movement   D = Double arm movement / T = Tension   M = slow-Motion

4. Without stepping, execute a RIGHT JEE-REU-GI (punch) to mid section. [S,N]

5. In a continuous motion, execute a LEFT JEE-REU-GI (punch) to the mid section [D,N].

N = No retraction   R = immediate **R**etraction / S = **S**ingle arm movement   D = **D**ouble arm movement / T = **T**ension   M = slow-**M**otion

6. Left foot adjusts to a RIGHT DUWEET-GOO-BEE SEO-GI (back stance) (facing east), execute a LEFT ADVANCED DOO-SOHN-NAHL MAHK-GI (double knifehand block). [D,N]

7.   Without stepping, execute a WEON DOO-SOHN-NAHL AH-RAE MAHK-GI (circular double knifehand low block). [D,N]

N = No retraction   R = immediate **Retraction** / S = Single arm movement   D = Double arm movement / T = Tension   M = slow-Motion

8.   Right foot advances forward executing a JEE KEO (foot stomp) ending in a JOO-CHOOM SEO-GI (middle stance) with the body facing north and eyes looking east).

The insert to the right shows the final position of the jee keo (foot stomp) and the proper chamber of the hand in preparation for the next move.

9. Without stepping, execute a RIGHT DEUNG JU-MEOK CHI-GI (backfist strike) toward the east (high section). [S,R]

N = No retraction   R = immediate **Retraction** / S = **S**ingle arm movement   D = **D**ouble arm movement / T = **T**ension   M = slow-**M**otion

10. Stepping left foot to right foot, execute a RIGHT YEOP CHAH-GI SAHM-BEON (#3 side kick) toward the east.

11. Place the right foot down next to the left into a GOOB-EUN MO-AH SEO-GI (low closed stance) facing the north. Execute a RIGHT UI/AH-RAE MAHK-GI (high/low block). [D,N]

N = No retraction   R = immediate **Retraction** / S = Single arm movement   D = **D**ouble arm movement / T = **T**ension   M = slow-**M**otion

12. Without stepping, execute a LEFT UI/AH-RAE MAHK-GI (high/low block). [D,N]

13. Right foot steps toward the north into a LEFT BEOM SEO-GI (rear stance), execute a RIGHT SOHN-NAHL AH-RAE MAHK-GI (knifehand low block). [S,M,N]

N = No retraction   R = immediate **Retraction** / S = **S**ingle arm movement   D = **D**ouble arm movement / T = **T**ension   M = slow-**M**otion

14. Execute a RIGHT AHP CHAH-GI IL-BEON (#1 front kick). Place the foot down in a JOO-CHOOM SEO-GI (middle stance) with the body facing west and eyes to the north.

15. Left foot moves to the right into a MO-AH SEO-GI (closed stance). Execute a RIGHT DDEE-EO NAHK-AH CHAH-GI IL-BEON (#1 jump hook kick) to the north.

N = No retraction   R = immediate **Retraction** / S = Single arm movement   **D** = **D**ouble arm movement / **T** = **T**ension   **M** = slow-**M**otion

16. Land in a RIGHT GYEO-ROO-GI SEO-GI (sparring stance) (to north) and execute a RIGHT KOO-JAH MAHK-GI (9-block). [D,N]

17. Double step (left foot to right, right steps out) to JOO-CHOOM SEO-GI (middle stance), with right toe and left heel on east-west line. Execute a RIGHT DOO-AHN PAHL-MOK MAHK-GI (double inner-forearm block). [D,N]

N = No retraction   R = immediate **Retraction** / S = Single arm movement   D = Double arm movement / T = Tension   M = slow-Motion

18. Without stepping, execute a LEFT JAE-CHYEO JEE-REU-GI (upset punch) to the high section. [S,R]

19. Without stepping, execute a RIGHT JAE-CHYEO BAH-TAHNG SOHN MAHK-GI (upset palm block). [S,N]

N = No retraction   R = immediate **R**etraction / S = Single arm movement   **D** = **D**ouble arm movement / T = Tension   M = slow-**M**otion

20. Without stepping, execute a LEFT JEE-REU-GI (punch) to mid section. [S,N]

21. In a continuous motion, execute a RIGHT JEE-REU-GI (punch) to the mid section. [D,N]

Ki-hap (yell).

N = No retraction   R = immediate **Retraction** / S = Single arm movement   D = Double arm movement / T = Tension   M = slow-Motion

22. Right foot adjusts to a LEFT DUWEET-GOO-BEE SEO-GI (back stance) toward the west), execute a RIGHT ADVANCED DOO-SOHN-NAHL MAHK-GI (double knifehand block). [D,N]

23. Without stepping, execute a WEON DOO-SOHN-NAHL AH-RAE MAHK-GI (circular double knifehand low block). [D,N]

N = No retraction   R = immediate Retraction / S = Single arm movement   D = Double arm movement / T = Tension   M = slow-Motion

24. Left foot advances forward executing a JEE KEO (foot stomp) ending in a JOO-CHOOM SEO-GI (middle stance) with the body facing north and eyes looking west.

The insert to the right shows the final position of the jee keo (foot stomp) and the proper chamber of the hand in preparation for the next move.

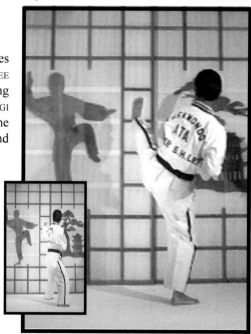

25. Without stepping, execute a LEFT DEUNG JU-MEOK CHI-GI (backfist strike) toward the west (high section). [S,R]

N = No retraction   R = immediate **Retraction** / S = Single arm movement   D = Double arm movement / T = Tension   M = slow-Motion

26. Stepping right foot to left foot, execute a YEOP CHAH-GI SAHM-BEON (#3 side kick) toward the west.

27. Place the left foot down next to the right into a GOOB-EUN MO-AH SEO-GI (low closed stance) facing the north. Execute a LEFT EOT-GEOL MAHK-GI (X-block) to the low section. [D,N]

N = No retraction R = immediate **Retraction** / S = Single arm movement D = Double arm movement / T = Tension M = slow-Motion

28. Without stepping, execute a two hand MOK-TEOL-ME JAB-KEE (head grab) toward the north.

29. Execute a RIGHT MOO-REUP CHI-GI (knee strike), bringing the hands down to meet the upward motion of the knee. Replace the foot next to the left foot.

N = No retraction   **R** = immediate **Retraction** / **S** = Single arm movement   **D** = Double arm movement / **T** = Tension   **M** = slow-**M**otion

30. Turn counterclockwise to a RIGHT BEOM SEO-GI (rear stance), execute a LEFT SOHN-NAHL AH-RAE MAHK-GI (knifehand low block) toward the south. [S,T,N]

31. Execute a LEFT AHP CHAH-GI IL-BEON (#1 front kick). Place the foot down in a JOO-CHOOM SEO-GI (middle stance) with the body facing west and eyes to south.

N = No retraction   R = immediate **Retraction** / S = Single arm movement   D = Double arm movement / T = Tension   M = slow-Motion

32. Right foot moves to the left into a MO-AH SEO-GI (closed stance). Execute a LEFT DDEE-EO NAHK-AH CHAH-GI IL-BEON (#1 jump hook kick) to the south.

33. Land in a LEFT GYEO-ROO-GI SEO-GI (sparring stance). Execute a LEFT KOO-JAH MAHK-GI (9-block) toward the south. [D,N]

N = No retraction   R = immediate **Retraction** / S = Single arm movement   D = Double arm movement / T = Tension   M = slow-Motion

34. Right foot steps toward south into a LEFT DUWEET-GOO-BEE SEO-GI (back stance). Execute a JONG-HAHP SAH-GAHK MAHK-GI (compound square block) with a left fist and right knifehand. [D,N]

35. Without stepping, (eyes to east) execute a RIGHT JAE-CHYEO SOHN-NAHL CHI-GI (knifehand strike) toward east. The LEFT UI MAHK-GI (high block) remains in place during this chi-gi (strike). [S,N]

N = No retraction   R = immediate **Retraction** / S = Single arm movement   D = Double arm movement / T = Tension   M = slow-Motion

36. Right foot adjusts to a RIGHT AHP-GOO-BEE SEO-GI (front stance), execute a LEFT BAHN-DAE SAE-WOON JEE-REU-GI (reverse vertical punch) toward the south (mid section). [S,N]

37. Execute a RIGHT DDEE-EO AHP CHAH-GI SAHM-BEON (#3 jump front kick) toward the south.

N = No retraction   R = immediate **Retraction** / S = Single arm movement   D = Double arm movement / T = Tension   M = slow-Motion

38. Land in a RIGHT AHP-GOO-BEE SEO-GI (front stance), execute a BAHN-DAE BAH-TAHNG SOHN CHI-GI (reverse palm strike) toward the south (high section). [S,N]

39. Right foot steps to left foot into a MO-AH SEO-GI (closed stance) with the body facing the east and the eyes to the south. Execute a RIGHT AHN-JOHK PAHL-MOK MAHK-GI (inward inner-forearm block) toward the south. [S,N]

N = No retraction   R = immediate **Retraction** / S = Single arm movement   D = Double arm movement / T = Tension   M = slow-Motion

40. Left foot moves counterclockwise to a JOO-CHOOM SEO-GI (middle stance) with the body facing west and the eyes to the south. Execute a LEFT SOO-PYEONG DUWEET-PAHL-GOOP CHI-GI (hor. back elbow strike) toward the south (high section). [S,N]

41. Without stepping, execute a LEFT SOHN-NAHL CHI-GI (knifehand strike) toward south. [S,N]

Ki-hap (yell).

N = No retraction   R = immediate **Retraction** /   S = **S**ingle arm movement   D = **D**ouble arm movement /   T = **T**ension   M = slow-**M**otion

42. Right foot steps to the left foot into a MO-AH SEO-GI (closed stance) facing the south. Execute an EOT-GEOL MAHK-GI (X-block) to the high section. [D,N]

43. Without stepping, execute a LEFT SOHN-NAHL CHI-GI (knifehand strike) toward the south (high section). [S,N]

N = No retraction   R = immediate **Retraction** / S = Single arm movement   **D** = **D**ouble arm movement / **T** = **T**ension   **M** = slow-**M**otion

44. LEFT MOO-REUP CHI-GI (knee strike) to left hand (meet at solar-plexus level). Place left foot down to right foot.

45. Right foot steps toward west to LEFT BEOM SEO-GI (rear stance). Execute a RIGHT EOP-EUN SOHN-NAHL MAHK-GI (ridgehand block) to the high section. [S,T,N]

N = No retraction   R = immediate **Retraction** / S = Single arm movement   D = Double arm movement / T = Tension   M = slow-Motion

46. Without stepping, execute a RIGHT SOHN-GEUT JEE-REU-GI (fingertip thrust) toward the west (high section). [S,M,N]

47. Left foot steps forward one-half stance length, RIGHT DOL-AH NAHK-AH CHAH-GI (spin hook kick).

The insert to the left shows the beginning of the clockwise motion prior to executing the chah-gi (kick).

N = No retraction   R = immediate **Retraction** / S = Single arm movement   D = **D**ouble arm movement / T = Tension   M = slow-Motion

48. Land in a JOO-CHOOM SEO-GI (middle stance) (body north, eyes west), execute a LEFT AH-RAE MAHK-GI (low block) toward the west. [S,N]

49. Without stepping, execute a LEFT AHN PAHL-MOK MAHK-GI (inner-fore-arm block) toward the west (high section). [S,N]

N = No retraction   R = immediate **Retraction** / S = Single arm movement   D = Double arm movement / T = Tension   M = slow-Motion

50. Without stepping, execute a LEFT JEE-REU-GI (punch) toward the west (mid section). [S,N]

51. Right foot steps to the left foot into a MO-AH SEO-GI (closed stance). Execute a LEFT YEOP CHAH-GI IL-BEON (#1 side kick) to the low section. [T,M]

N = No retraction   R = immediate **Retraction** / S = **S**ingle arm movement   D = **D**ouble arm movement / T = **T**ension   M = slow-**M**otion

52. Execute a double (movements 52 & 53) LEFT DOL-RYEO CHAH-GI (round kick). First, a LEFT DOL-RYEO CHAH-GI (round kick) to the mid section...

53. ...then, a LEFT DOL-
RYEO CHAH-GI (round kick)
to the high section.

N = No retraction   R = immediate **Retraction** / S = Single arm movement   D = Double arm movement / T = Tension   M = slow-Motion

54. Land in a LEFT GYEO-
ROO-GI SEO-GI (sparring
stance) toward the west.
Execute a LEFT JONG-HAHP
DOO-AH-RAE   MAHK-GI
(compound double low
block) toward the west
with left knifehand and
right fist. [D,N]

55. Step right foot to left. Then turn 270 degrees counterclockwise into a RIGHT DUWEET-GOO-BEE SEO-GI (back stance) toward the north. Execute a JONG-HAHP SAH-GAHK MAHK-GI (compound square block) with a right fist and left knifehand. [D,N]

The insert to the left shows the proper chamber of the hands and the body position as the turn is in progress.

N = No retraction   R = immediate **Retraction**   /   S = **S**ingle arm movement   **D** = **D**ouble arm movement   /   T = **T**ension   M = slow-**M**otion

56. Without stepping, (eyes to east) execute a LEFT JAE-CHYEO SOHN-NAHL CHI-GI (knifehand strike) toward east. The RIGHT UI MAHK-GI (high block) remains in place during this chi-gi (strike). [S,N]

57. Left foot adjusts to a LEFT AHP-GOO-BEE SEO-GI (front stance), execute a RIGHT BAHN-DAE SAE-WOON JEE-REU-GI (reverse vertical punch) toward the north (mid section). [S,N]

N = No retraction   R = immediate **R**etraction / **S** = **S**ingle arm movement   **D** = **D**ouble arm movement / **T** = **T**ension   **M** = slow-**M**otion

58. Execute a LEFT DDEE-EO AHP CHAH-GI SAHM-BEON (#3 jump front kick).

59. Land in a LEFT AHP-GOO-BEE SEO-GI (front stance), execute a RIGHT BAHN-DAE BAH-TAHNG SOHN CHI-GI (reverse palm strike) toward the north (high section). [S,N]

N = No retraction   R = immediate **Retraction** / S = Single arm movement   D = Double arm movement / T = Tension   M = slow-Motion

60. Left foot steps to right foot into a MO-AH SEO-GI (closed stance) with the body facing east and the eyes to the north. Execute a LEFT AHN-JOHK PAHL-MOK MAHK-GI (inward inner-forearm block) toward the north.

61. Right foot moves clockwise to a JOO-CHOOM SEO-GI (middle stance) (body west, eyes to north). Execute a RIGHT SOO-PYEONG DUWEET-PAHL-GOOP CHI-GI (hor. back elbow strike) toward the north (high section). [S,N]

Ki-hap (yell).

N = No retraction   R = immediate **Retraction** / S = Single arm movement   D = Double arm movement / T = Tension   M = slow-Motion

62. Without stepping, execute a RIGHT SOHN-NAHL CHI-GI (knifehand strike) toward north. [S,N]

63. Left foot steps to the right foot (turning counterclockwise toward the south) into a GOOP-EUN MO-AH SEO-GI (low closed stance). Execute a LEFT UI/AH-RAE SOHN-NAHL MAHK-GI (high/low knifehand block). [D,N]

N = No retraction   **R** = immediate **Retraction** / **S** = Single arm movement   **D** = **D**ouble arm movement / **T** = Tension   **M** = slow-**M**otion

64. Without stepping, execute a RIGHT UI/AH-RAE SOHN-NAHL MAHK-GI (high/low knifehand block) to south. [D,N]

65. Left foot steps toward east to RIGHT BEOM SEO-GI (rear stance). Execute a LEFT EOP-EUN SOHN-NAHL MAHK-GI (ridgehand block) to the high section. [S,T,N]

N = No retraction   R = immediate **Retraction** / S = Single arm movement   D = Double arm movement / T = Tension   M = slow-Motion

66. Without stepping, execute a LEFT SOHN-GEUT JEE-REU-GI (fingertip thrust) to the high section. [S,M,N]

67. Right foot steps forward one-half stance length, LEFT DOL-AH NAHK-AH CHAH-GI (spin hook kick).

The insert to the left shows the practitioner as he has progressed partially through the turn.

N = **N**o retraction   **R** = immediate **Retraction** / S = **S**ingle arm movement   **D** = **D**ouble arm movement / **T** = **T**ension   **M** = slow-**M**otion

68. Land in a JOO-CHOOM SEO-GI (middle stance) (body north, eyes east), execute a RIGHT AH-RAE MAHK-GI (low block) toward the east. [S,N]

69. Without stepping, execute a RIGHT AHN PAHL-MOK MAHK-GI (inner-forearm block) to the high section. [S,N]

N = No retraction   R = immediate **Retraction** / S = Single arm movement   D = Double arm movement / T = Tension   M = slow-Motion

70. Without stepping, execute a RIGHT JEE-REU-GI (punch) toward the east (mid section). [S,N]

71. Left foot steps to the right foot into a MO-AH SEO-GI (closed stance). Execute a RIGHT YEOP CHAH-GI IL-BEON (#1 side kick) to the low section. [T,M]

N = No retraction   R = immediate **Retraction** / S = **S**ingle arm movement   D = **D**ouble arm movement / T = **T**ension   M = slow-**M**otion

72. Execute a double (movements 72 & 73) RIGHT DOL-RYEO CHAH-GI (round kick). First, a RIGHT DOL-RYEO CHAH-GI (round kick) to the mid section...

73. ...then, a RIGHT DOL-RYEO CHAH-GI (round kick) to the high section.

N = No retraction   R = immediate **Retraction**   /   S = Single arm movement   D = Double arm movement   /   T = Tension   M = slow-Motion

74. Land in a RIGHT GYEO-ROO-GI SEO-GI (sparring stance) to the east, execute a LEFT JONG-HAHP DOO-AH-RAE MAHK-GI (compound double low block) with a left fist and right knifehand. [D,N]

75. Left foot steps forward one seo-gi (stance) length. Execute a RIGHT DDEE-EO YEOP CHAH-GI EE-BEON (#2 jump side kick) toward the east.

N = No retraction   R = immediate **Retraction** / S = Single arm movement   **D** = Double arm movement / **T** = Tension   **M** = slow-Motion

76. Land in a LEFT DUWEET-GOO-BEE SEO-GI (back stance). Execute an ADVANCED DOO-BAH-KAHT PAHL-MOK MAHK-GI (double outer-forearm block) toward the east. [D,N]

77. Without stepping, execute a LEFT BAHN-DAE JEE-REU-GI (reverse punch) to the mid section.

N = No retraction   R = immediate **Retraction** / S = Single arm movement   D = Double arm movement / T = Tension   M = slow-Motion

78. Without stepping, execute a WEON DOO-BAH-KAHT PAHL-MOK MAHK-GI (circular double outer-forearm block) toward the east. [D,N]

79. Right foot steps back (counterclockwise) to a RIGHT DUWEET-GOO-BEE SEO-GI (back stance). Execute an ADVANCED DOO-BAH-KAHT PAHL-MOK MAHK-GI (double outer-forearm block) toward the east.

The insert to the left shows progress of the turn as the practitioner lifts the right leg and places it into a right duweet-goo-bee seo-gi (back stance) as seen in the larger photo.

N = No retraction   R = immediate **Retraction** / S = Single arm movement   D = **D**ouble arm movement / T = Tension   M = slow-Motion

80. Without stepping, execute a RIGHT BAHN-DAE JEE-REU-GI (reverse punch) to the mid section. [S,N]

81. Without stepping, execute a WEON DOO-BAH-KAHT PAHL-MOK MAHK-GI (circular double outer-forearm block) toward the east. [D,N]

N = No retraction   R = immediate **Retraction** / S = Single arm movement   D = Double arm movement / T = Tension   M = slow-Motion

BAHN JEE-DO-JAH JAH-SAE
(Half-command Position)

Move the left foot back to a NAH-RAHN-HEE SEO-GI (parallel stance).

Assume this position on the command, "BAH-RO (end)"

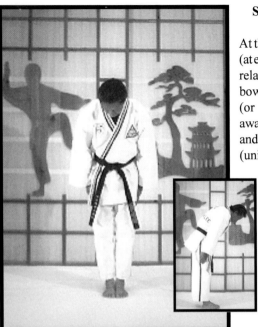

SHI-UH (At Ease)

At the command, "shi-uh (at ease)," the student may relax. The student should bow, say "thank you, sir (or ma'am)," then turn away from the senior rank and straighten the do-bok (uniform) or tend to other immediate needs.

Note that in the insert to the left, the back is curved as Chief Master Lee bows.

SHI-UH JAH-SAE (At Ease Position)

Turn back quickly and stand in a SHI-UH JAH-SAE (at ease) position. This is the end of ShimJun and the student is now prepared for the next directive.

MASTER
MAL KUN
LEE

6th Degree
Tae-sah Nim

MASTER
GYUNG KUN
LEE

6th Degree
Tae-sah Nim

At the black belt level, there are no preassigned il-bo gyeo-roo-gi (1-step sparring), or gyeo-roo-gi boo-boon (sparring segments). Black belts are encouraged to be creative and develop combinations of skills. These combinations are displayed as part of special demonstrations and ceremonies.

However, a part of gyeo-roo-gi (sparring) that does take on a new look is competition. At the black belt level, you can compete toward a competition rank in your national association or even in the world. This is called the

"Top Ten."

NATIONAL "TOP TEN":

There are four levels of ranking in competition among black belts: you can rank in your school (optional, controlled by local school), rank in your region (optional, controlled by Regional Chief of Tournaments), rank in your national organization (controlled by National Chairman of Tournaments), and ranked worldwide (controlled by WTTU Chairman of Tournaments).

This ranking is done on a points system. The following are the rules concerning ranking in the "Top Ten."

Junior Top Ten

The age of the child on January 1st will decide in what division his/her Top Ten points will be awarded for the entire shee-hahp (tournament) year. If the child will turn 17 before January 1st he should compete in the adult division all year. If he competes as a junior while he is 16 and an adult when he becomes 17, the points earned as a junior will not carry over into the adult division. Please note that all junior divisions are based only on age. There is no separation by rank in the junior Top Ten. The regional competition divisions should be made as fair and competitive as possible. In regionals, children must be divided by age and size. Division size must also be considered in order to be competitive.

Adult, VIP, Executive, and Silver Top Ten

The age of the competitor on January 1 will decide which division he/she may compete in. The age groups for competition will be as follows:

17-25 Adult; 26-35 VIP; 36-49 Executive; 50 & up Silver

As an example, if the competitor is 36 before January 1st, then they should compete in the Executive division for the entire year, beginning with the World Championship the previous June. Points for one rank division may not be carried over into the next higher division. VIP, Executive or Silver competitors who compete in the younger age divisions may transfer points into their correct age group. Adult competitors may not compete in the VIP or older age group unless combined by the Shee-hahp (tournament) director to achieve full divisions. Regional shee-hahp (tournaments) may combine age groups to achieve full point divisions. Silver division competitors will not be separated by rank, only age. All ranks will compete in a single division unless there are more than sixteen competitors.

Cho Dan Yae-bee (1st Degree Rec.) Black Belt

Because there is a great difference in difficulty between Choong Jung #2 and ShimJun, cho dan yae-bee (1st degree rec.) students may compete with red belts if they wish. They will not receive Top Ten points in the red belt division. If they wish to compete for Top Ten points, they must compete with the cho dan (1st degree) decided competitors. The choice of division will be made by the competitor and his sah-bum nim (instructor). However, they may only compete in one division per shee-hahp (tournament).

Rank Change

If an adult competitor is promoted to higher rank during the tournament year, except at the World Championships National Black Belt Shim-sah (testing) (see Tournament Point Accumulation), he will not be allowed to carry over points to higher rank division (for .point accumulation, see first paragraph of "Junior Top Ten" on previous page). If a 16 year old is promoted to sahm dan (3rd degree), he must compete as an adult, and not with 15 and 16 year old cho dan (1st degree) and ee dan (2nd degree) Juniors. If he is promoted to sahm dan (3rd degree) after the regular competition year, does not compete in any adult divisions, and carries enough points to remain in the Top Ten, he can keep his points for year end recognition only if he does not compete at the new rank.

It is recommended that any adult Black Belt who will be shim-sah (testing) during the tournament year (from World Championships through the final April shee-hahp (tournaments)) compete in the next rank division. This will assure that all points earned toward Top Ten placement will be accrued in one division. For example, a cho dan (1st degree) student is eligible to test in January for ee dan yae-bee (2nd degree rec.) and is interested in competing for Top Ten. It would be to his benefit to begin competing in the ee dan (2nd degree) divisions at Regional and National shee-hahp (tournaments). Anyone who wishes to follow this plan needs to tell the Tournament Director at each regional competition in advance so that his judging assignments will not conflict with the competition times. Ee dan yae-bee (2nd degree rec.) Black belts are to compete with the ee dan (2nd degree) black belts for the purpose of compiling points. If the cho dan (1st degree) and ee dan (2nd degree) divisions are combined, points will be awarded. If an ee dan (2nd degree) division is available, no points will be awarded to an ee dan (2nd degree) who competes in a cho dan (1st degree) division. Any black belt may compete in the next higher rank division at his discretion.

Divisions

Top Ten points are pro-rated for small divisions. If there are not enough competitors to make a full Top Ten division with at least 5 people, divisions may be combined for competition. No more than 2 different Top Ten divisions can be combined for competition. For example: cho dan (1st degree) and ee dan (2nd degree) Black Belts, ee dan (2nd degree) and sahm dan (3rd degree) Black Belts, or sahm dan (3rd degree) and sah dan (4th degree) Black Belts. Other examples: Adult cho dan (1st degree) Black Belt and VIP cho dan (1st degree) Black Belt, or Adult Women ee dan (2nd degree) Black Belt and VIP Women sahm dan (3rd degree) Black Belt. If any other type of division is made at a regional shee-hahp (tournament), other than specified above, the Regional Chief of Tournaments or the Tournament Host will notify the Songahm Taekwondo Headquarters staff or the National Chairman of Tournaments, so that Top Ten points are given to the competitors in a combined division, and will be carried over into the competitors appropriate Top Ten division. On a regional level, at the Regional Directors discretion, sah dan (4th degree) Adult or VIP Men's and Women's divisions may be combined. National level shee-hahp (tournaments) will remain separate.

Tournament Point Accumulation

A competitor may accumulate a total of 90 points during the tournament year. He will receive double points from the World Championships and one national shee-hahp (tournament). A competitor may participate in both Nationals, Fall and Spring, but he may use points from only one toward his Top Ten total. A competitor testing for higher rank during the National Black Belt testing at World Championships who is promoted, will be allowed to carry points earned during that shee-hahp (tournament) only toward their new Top Ten division.

A competitor will receive single points from his best 5 regional shee-hahp (tournaments), no matter how many they attend within or outside their region. If a competitor has an expired membership, points will be tabulated in the computer file but the competitor will not be listed in the Top Ten file nor will they be allowed to compete for the Championship if the renewal was not received prior to the end of the tournament year (late April). Any certified sah-bum nim (instructor) who is a Top Ten competitor must have a current certification or the same will apply. If the sah-bum nim (instructor) will file a "letter of intent" stating the date of the camp he plans to attend for recertification, his expiration date will be extended for 12 months from receipt of letter. This type of extension will be allowed only once.

Pro-rated Points for Small Divisions			
	Points awarded for:		
# of Competitors	1st Place	2nd Place	3rd Place
5+	5	3	1
4	4	3	1
3	3	2	1
2	2	1	
1	1		

MASTER
RICHARD
ANDERSON

6th Degree
Tae-sah Nim

MASTER
ROBERT
JAGER

6th Degree
Tae-sah Nim

Obviously you have now completed what was probably your most difficult and stressful shim-sah (testing) of your training. This shim-sah (testing) was probably as much pressure as when you stood as a white belt ready to test for orange belt. Look how far you have traveled down this path. You have truly persevered through the Taekwondo path known as "The Way."

There are many new requirements that will be covered in this chapter. A black belt takes on new requirements and new responsibilities. This chapter is designed to help you understand what will be expected of you as a cho dan (1st degree) black belt as you prepare to test toward ee dan (2nd degree) black belt.

CHO DAN SHIM-SAH (1ST DEGREE TESTING):

심 사

Your next shim-sah (testing) will be your opportunity to demonstrate the basic skills you have developed over a year of time as a black belt. Although the shim-sah (testing) procedure may not be much different from that of the shim-sah (testing) for cho dan (1st degree) black belt, the expectations that the judges panel have are more critical.

RANK PROMOTIONAL SHIM-SAH (TESTING):

As a result of successfully testing from cho dan yae-bee (1st degree rec.) black belt to cho dan (1st degree) black belt, you should have received your cho dan (1st degree) black with the following inscriptions:

In special cases, the "association name" is replaced with a special inscription such as "pil-sung" which means "victory."

The box on the left side of the belt (see above diagram) has a single bar in it representing the rank of cho dan (1st degree).

At your next rank shim-sah (testing), you will be required to perform ShimJun Poome-sae (form), spar a minimum of two times, and break the required combinations of boards (see board breaking later in this chapter).

IMPORTANT NOTE: Black belts are not allowed to repeat a poome-sae (form) during shim-sah (testing). Failure to complete the poome-sae (form) correctly on the first attempt will result in a failure.

The cho dan (1st degree) black belt is scored on poome-sae (form), gyeo-roo-gi (sparring), and board breaking. A student who performs with "excellence" will receive a score of "90"; performing good will receive a score of "80"; average receives a "70"; and, poor execution or an incomplete poome-sae (form) receives a "60."

The scores given for poome-sae (form), gyeo-roo-gi (sparring), and board breaking are added together and your advancement is based on the average given by all certified judges. Some sah-bum nim (Instructors) ask questions during shim-sah (testing) and some require additional exercises (such as lower ranked poome-sae [forms], special demonstrations, etc.).

Two or more certified sah-bum nim (Instructors) are required for promotional shim-sah (testings). It is also required that a guest sah-bum nim (Instructor) be present when possible. The senior sah-bum nim (Instructor) must be at least two ranks higher than the rank the black belt is testing for.

The areas that are observed in scoring a poome-sae (form) are: memorization, proper execution of *technique (see pg. 26), presentation, flow, attitude, appearance, respect, courtesy, enthusiasm, confidence, self-control, eye contact, proper breathing, speed, and power.

Following the shim-sah (testing), you can usually expect one week or less to pass prior to receiving your results. This allows the national headquarters time to process all results and issue certificates registering your rank internationally.

There are fees that must be paid in order to cover administration costs. All fees are based on standards set by the world headquarters, but may be forced to vary due to the local economy and cost of business operations.
The fees for shim-sah (testing) cover the cost of international registration of rank, certificate, rank insignias (belt, etc.), location costs, and guest sah-bum nim's (Instructor's) expenses.

*techniques on previous page are evaluated on the following criteria:

seo-gi (stances) = width, length, knee bend, weight distribution.

chah-gi (kicks) = chamber (includes pivot and solid sole -- flat stable footing), execution (includes: foot position, posture and hand position), re-chamber and return.

chi-gi (strikes) and mahk-gi (blocks) = start position, full extension (includes: arm rotation, direction, timing, posture and coordination) and ending position.

BOARD BREAKING OPTIONS:

The following is a list of breaking options for a cho-dan (1st degree) black belt shim-sah (testing) for ee-dan (2nd degree) black belt.

All breaks should be done as "combinations" -- as though in a combat situation. After bowing, the black belt should break immediately. Stopping to "measure" the boards or other pauses longer than taking a breath shall be considered a "try" and will count against the black belt's score.

Black belts may not repeat the same break in two consecutive shim-sah (testing) (regardless of length of time in between the shim-sah [testings]).

Size

The size of the board is to be determined as follows (*may be determined at sah-bum nim's [instructor's] descretion):

Child (6 yrs. and under)	5" X 12"
Child (7 & 8 yrs.)	7" X 12"
Child (9 & 10 yrs.)	9" X 12"
Child (11 & 12 yrs.)	11" X 12" (1 board)
Youth (13 & older)	11" X 12" (*1 or 2 bds)
Adult (18 & older)	11" X 12" (*2 boards)

Number of Boards

The number of boards used is dependent upon age, sex, and personal integrity (or that of your sah-bum nim [instructor]). Women and children are only required to use one board (of the proper size) at each station. However, women are encouraged to use two boards if they are as consistant as the male students with the same technique (personal integrity is of the utmost importance). To use only one board to ensure that you "pass" a test is not only unfair to others, but is cheating yourself from achieving your personal best.

Sah dan (4th degree) and higher black belt men should break two boards on all techniques except yeop chah-gi (side kicks) which require three boards. Again, women of this rank must use personal integrity in choosing the number of boards to be used. In some cases, the judges may require an additional board at all stations based on skill and size of the black belt.

Speed Breaks

Nahk-ah chah-gi (hook kicks) and heel kicks may be done supported or as speed breaks where indicated. Speed breaks require the use of one board. However, at higher skill levels, two boards may be required.

Obstacles

Obstacles must consist of people approximately your own size. Each person is to bend over at the waist with the knees only slightly bent. There <u>must</u> be a one person space between your obstacle and the board/s. This space does not count as one of your obstacles.

Re-attempts

Up to three attempts may be tried to complete a series of breaks. However, after each attempt, all stations must be reset and the breaks must be completed as a combination. In the case of an obstacle jump; a black belt may not be given a third attempt if it becomes obvious that he/she cannot clear the obstacles and is causing potential danger to the volunteers.

Technical Requirements

Cho dan (1st degree) shim-sah (testing) for Ee dan (2nd degree).

Option 1:
    Sohn-nahl chi-gi (knifehand strike)
    Ddee-eo yeop chah-gi (jump side kick) over two obstacles
Option 2:
    Jee-reu-gi (punch -- lunge or reverse)
    Dol-ryeo chah-gi (round kick) to face level
    Yeop chah-gi (side kick) to mid section
Option 3:
    Jae-chyeo sohn-nahl chi-gi (upset knifehand strike)
    Ddee-eo bahn-dae yeop chah-gi (jump reverse side kick)
Option 4:
    Ahp chah-gi (front kick)
    Yeop chah-gi (side kick)
    Dol-ryeo chah-gi (round kick)
      (note: one kick must be with the opposite leg)

NOTE: Sah-bum nim (instructors) of students with special physical handicaps may make adjustments on technique requirements after consulting with the National Chairman of Testings.

SONGAHM RANK SYSTEM:

The "rank system" of Songahm Taekwondo is painted with a variety of symbols and philosophy. There is almost nothing within the system for which there cannot be found a historical, philosophical or modern meaning and purpose. Following, are explanations behind some of the prominent and some of the hidden symbols among the cho dan (1st degree) level.

For any laymen of Taekwondo that has at least learned how to count in Korean (both the ancient and modern systems), it would become obvious that the Korean name for a first degree black belt "cho dan" seems to be inconsistent with the others (i.e.: ee-dan, sam-dan, etc.). Why is the first degree not called an "*il*-dan" or "*hah-nah*-dan" both prefixes of which represent the number one. As a matter of fact, the Korean word "cho" does not even represent a number. Instead, it simply means "beginner." In essence, "cho dan" means the "beginner degree" and not the first degree.

People outside of the martial arts are often confused by the interpretation of this rank, "first degree," because the term first usually denotes the highest place (i.e.: first place, first in line, etc.). It should be noted that often we refer to first in a lesser or basic meaning. For example, a baby takes his "first" step. This is hardly his best step. Or, in order to climb a ladder, you must take the first step. And, in order to take a journey of a thousand miles, you must take the first step. This is how the word "first" is applied to a cho dan (1st degree) black belt. In the Korean language it is clearly understood that the first degree is the beginner of the black belt levels...thus, "cho dan."

At the color belt levels, you were learning the different attributes of Taekwondo. At the black belt level, you are learning to apply these attributes in all aspects of your life.

You are now "planting seeds" that will determine the crop you will one day harvest. You are at the beginning of the season to sow.

If you sow great things, you will harvest great things. If you sow second best, you can only be second best. And, if you sow seeds of mastering the many areas of your life, then one day, you will harvest a "Master." Visions of your future have been planted in your mind. Now, it is time to nourish these visions and strive for perfection.

Black belt does not mean expert. It is one striving toward the level of expert. Even the Shim-jun Poome-sae is 81 moves of colored belt technique with a new flair. The poome-sae (form) is executed differently but with some basic and advanced color belt moves. This is a time to refresh your mind and review your technique. It is like your freshman year of college. It is a time allotted to prepare you for the hard but rewarding road ahead.

Shim-jun Poome-sae

This poome-sae (form) is almost double the number of moves found in your previous forms. The purpose behind this is to increase your memorization skills, stamina, concentration, and to add a level of difficulty. It will also increase your coordination due to the new "single-hand" techniques.

To attempt to execute ShimJun with the same intensity as you performed your previous poome-sae (forms), or with the energy expended by the use of controlled reaction-force, would result in a quick exhaustion of your body and mind. ShimJun is designed to flow smoothly from one technique to the next. It should almost look like a graceful display of rhythmic technique. Many people today try to add power and "snap" to each move. This in itself looks exciting to the layman, but to the mature martial artist, there is a realization of the power and devastation behind speed, flow, and timing.

This "newness" you will experience in the execution of this poome-sae (form) should bring a sense of pride as you realize you have passed over the bridge to a new shore of learning. You are set apart from the colors that you once wore around your waist and have matured into an "adult" of the Songahm Taekwondo system.

Stars and Bars

The stars and bars used in the rank system stem from the "martial" part of the martial arts. This system is based on the rank system used in the militaries of many different countries. In the following descriptions, we will use the United States Armed Forces for the comparison.

Why is it that stars are used for high ranking officials? This is because of the symbolism of power that the "star" has achieved. People "look toward the stars," as well as "reach for the stars." People that have achieved fame and popularity are called "stars" because they shine or stand out from others. The number of stars (1 to 5) increase with the level of recognition, influence, knowledge, and power.

Look at the following list of ranks and how the achievement of that rank is similar to that of the comparable military rank.

1R	First rec. black belt	(no bars)	**2nd Lieutenant**
1D	First dec. black belt	(1 bar)	**1st Lieutenant**
2R	Second rec. black belt	(1 bar)	**Captain**

(at this position, the officer is evaluated for promotion. success = promotion, failure = discharge or in TKD the student is returned to 1st degree dec.)

2D   Second rec. black belt (2 bars)   **Major**

3D   Third deg. black belt (3 bars)   **Lt. Colonel**

4D   Fourth deg. black belt (4 bars)   **Full Colonel**

(At this level, the government becomes involved and begins to evaluate the Full Colonel for the position of General. Even the Congress must review the candidate before there can be a promotion. In TKD, candidates for fourth degree and higher must be approved by a specially appointed board of examiners made up of Songahm Taekwondo Masters.)

5D   Fifth deg. black belt (1 star)   **1-star General**

6D   Sixth deg. black belt (2 stars)   **2-star General**

7D   Seventh deg. black belt (3 stars)   **3-star General**

8D   Eighth deg. black belt (4 stars)   **4-star General**

9D   Ninth deg. black belt (5 stars)   **5-star General**

(There can only be one ninth degree holding this position at any time. This Master is chosen from the candidates at eighth degree. Even the Korean name for the eighth degree master, "Jong-sah" means seed. From this seed will sprout a Grand Master. The same analogy can be found in the story of the BeeRyong (flying dragon) for which the Grand Master's staff, the BeeRyong Bong, is named. From all the dragons at the bottom of the lake (where they grow and develop), one with exceptional knowledge and skill is chosen and given the ability to fly. The BeeRyong rises from the depths of the lake and takes flight, bringing peace to mankind.)

NOTE: for the story of the BeeRyong, refer to the story in the Philosophy section of *Volume A: Philosophy and Traditions*.

The following is a flow chart describing the system behind the Songahm Taekwondo ranks. **# in pos.** = the number of people that can hold the rank at one time. **Degree** = the degree that the person holds in Taekwondo. **Rank** = the military rank on which the degree is based. **Combined forces** = how the groups are combined to make even larger groups. **# under command** = the estimated number of people that should be under the officers level of the chain of command.

# IN POS.	DEGREE	RANK	GROUPING	COMBINED FORCES	# UNDER COMMAND
1	9th	5-star Gen.	Mixed Elements (wartime)	Allied Force	Allied Supreme Commander 300,000 people
9	8th	4-star Gen.	Army group	2 or 3 corps	240,000 people
27	7th	3-star Gen.	Corp	2 or 3 armies	80,000 people
81	6th	2-star Gen.	Army	(variable)	40,000 people
180	5th	1-star Gen.	Division	7-8 Batallions	20,000 people
1800	4th	Full Colonel	Brigade	2-3 Batallions	6,160 - 7,040 people
no limit	3rd	Lt. Colonel	Battalion	5 Companies	198-880 people
no limit	2nd	Major	Company	3 or 4 Platoons	99-176 people
no limit	2nd rec.	Captain	(same as above)	(same as above)	99-176 people
no limit	1st	1st Lieutenant	Platoon	3 or 4 Squadrons	33 or 44 people
no limit	1st rec.	2nd Lieutenant	(same as above)	(same as above)	33 or 44 people

POOME-SAE (FORM) SYMBOLS:

ShimJun & JungYul Poome-sae:
(1st and 2nd Degrees)

INFINITY
Longevity
Loyalty
Knowledge

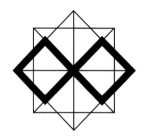

ChungSan, SokBong, & ChungHae Poome-sae:
(3rd, 4th, & 5th Degrees)

HOURGLASS
Begins to recognized
the importance of time
Learns to Master time

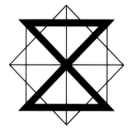

JhangSoo Poome-sae:
(6th Degrees)

STARBURST
Recognizable
Illuminates with knowledge

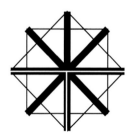

At this level, the Master is taught 66 of the 96 movements in the yook dan (6th degree) form. Because he is a Master now, he must begin to add to the art of Taekwondo. His knowledge gives him the privilege to write into the annals of Songahm. Thus, the final 30 movements are created by the Master; his personal touch on Songahm.

NOTE: The above Songahm stars have been rotated to show the emblem in its proper persepctive.

The actual pattern made in each form follows this design but may start in a different direction than what may seem to appear in the above symbols.

SHEE-HAHP (TOURNAMENTS):　시 합

At this level in your training, you should be very familiar with the rules and organization of Songahm Taekwondo shee-hahp (tournaments). Now however, with the rank of black belt comes a new responsibility. You must now prepare to sit as a judge of Taekwondo technique.

The following is a listing of requirements and qualifications to be a certified judge. This is not just a privilege, it is your responsibility to be available now to give back the time and effort that other judges gave you while you were a student.

Shee-hahp (tournament) Judging Certification

Level 1 Judge - This judge may be a corner judge for colored belt competition. This judge will receive a 1-inch wide blue chevron on the right sleeve of the uniform jacket. The chevron should be centered (on a diagonal) on the top crease of the right sleeve. The left edge (as you look at the uniform) should be two inches from the bottom of the sleeve and the right edge should be four inches from the sleeve bottom.

Requirements of Level 1 Judge -- He/she is to be at least 12 years of age, and a cho dan (1st degree) black belt decided or higher rank. Level 1 judges 12 years old may judge only competitors ages 12 and under, while under the supervision of two judges ages 16 or older.

Student level black belts must know all Songahm poome-sae (forms) and il-bo gyeo-roo-gi (1-step sparring) for white, orange, and yellow belts. It is highly recommended, before anyone certify for Level 1, that they have participated as a time and score keeper during one or more tournaments.

Level 2 Judge - This judge may be a center judge for colored belt rings and a corner judge for black belt rings. This judge will receive a 1-inch wide red chevron on the right sleeve of the do-bok (uniform) jacket. This will be placed 1/4 inch above the blue chevron.

Requirements of Level 2 - He/she is to be at least 14 years of age, and a cho dan (1st degree) black belt decided or higher rank. Level 2 judges 14 years of age may judge only competitors ages 14 and under, while under the supervision of two judges ages 16 or older.

Level 3 Judge - This judge may be center judge in Black Belt rings. This judge will receive a 1-inch wide black chevron on the right sleeve of the uniform top 1/4 inch above the red chevron.

Requirements of Level 3 - He/she is to be at least 16 years of age and an ee dan (2nd degree) black belt decided or higher rank.

For additional information about preparing for certification or the time and location of local shim-sah (testing) sites for certification, contact your sah-bum nim (Instructor) or the Regional Chief of Tournaments.

TAEKWONDO THEE (BELT): 태권도 띠

The Songahm Taekwondo cho dan (1st degree) wears a black belt with either the association name or special insignia on the right side and his/her name and rank on the left side. Black belts are double wrap.

The following is the meaning behind the black belt:

> # The tree has reached maturity and overcome the darkness[1].
> # It must now begin to plant seeds for the future.

1 = the colors of the spectrum are bound together and are not reflected off an object, resulting in the absence of light known as BLACK or darkness

The purpose of the black color in the thee (belt) is that the color black is created when all the colors of the light spectrum have been absorbed into an object. That object has "taken control" of the colors and retained them. If one color was to escape, the object would no longer be black. The student has mastered the nine grades of Taekwondo. He/she has absorbed all the knowledge of the color ranks and overcome or "mastered" that level of training.

DO-BOK (UNIFORM):   도 복

The do-bok (uniform) takes on a new look at the black belt level. Besides the black belt itself, the black belt must also place a one inch black stripe along the bottom of the do-bok (uniform) top or a one inch red stripe on the collar, depending on whether the black belt will continue training as a student only (black border stripe) or prepare toward being a certified sah-bum nim (instructor) under the Instructor Trainee program (red stripe). If the black belt is a junior and desires to prepare toward Instructor certification, he/she may join the Junior Leadership Program and wear a red, white, and blue collar stripe.

Also, if the black belt pursues the Junior Leadership Program or the Instructor Trainee Program, he/she will remove the city and state from the back of the do-bok (uniform) and replace it with his/her name. It is a requirement to have the proper lettering on the back of the do-bok (uniform). A uniform with no lettering is not an option for any black belt. The organization patch and local school patch (optional) must also be displayed on the do-bok (uniform).

As time goes on, you may also add special patches approved by your national organization to your do-bok (uniform). Also, chevrons for judging certification level may be added to the sleeves of your do-bok (uniform).

For information concerning history and philosophy see *Volume A*.

Rules For The Taekwondo Do-bok (Uniform):

1.   The do-bok (uniform) should not visibly display any manufacturer symbols or logos.

2. No pockets are to be apparent from the outside of the do-bok (uniform).
3. Sleeves must be full length.
4. Pants and sleeves may not be rolled up.
5. Left lapel always crosses over the right lapel.
6. An organization (WTTU, ATA, STF, etc.) patch and a school patch (optional) may be worn.
7. No trimming (such as stripes around the sleeves or pants) is allowed.
8. If the student's name is written or sewn on the do-bok (uniform), it must be done inside where it is not visible.
9. The do-bok (uniform) should not be worn for purposes other than Taekwondo related activity.

STUDENT OR TRAINEE?

"To be or not to be; that is the question." And that is the question you face as a new cho dan (1st degree). You must make a choice of which path to take. This choice does not have to be permanent, but nonetheless, must be made upon obtaining the new rank and responsibility of cho dan (1st degree). Your choice will be between taking the path of a student or that of a sah-bum nim (instructor) via the "Instructor Trainee" program. Juniors (ages 15 and under) are give the options of becoming a student or enrolling into the "Junior Trainee Instructor Program."

The following is a brief description of what each option you have entails.

Student Black Belt

The black belt that does not desire to become an instructor trainee or desire to pursue a career in Taekwondo can choose to remain a "student" black belt. This option has much less responsibility yet retains most black belt privileges.

If you choose this option, you will be required to wear a one inch black border around the bottom hem of you do-bok (uniform). You will also be required to wear the name of your city and state on the back of your uniform with the other traditional lettering (only boo sah-bum nim [trainees] and sah-bum nim [instructors] are permitted to wear their name on the back of their do-bok [uniform]).

Boo Sah-bum Nim (Trainee Instructor)

The boo sah-bum nim is the path that must be taken if you are 16 or older and desire to become a class assistant, sah-bum nim (instructor), club owner or school owner (Taekwondo career).

To become a part of the program, you simply must simply receive your instructor's permission, meet the basic require-ments, and send a completed application to the World Head-quarters. You then begin to fulfill the requirements that will need to be eligible to test for certification as a Songahm Taekwondo Sah-bum nim (instructor).

Junior Trainee Instructor Program (JTIP)

The JTIP program is for youth between the ages of 11 and 15 who desire to be a Songahm Taekwondo Sah-bum nim (instructor). There are few requirements to becoming a part of the program. See your instructor for details.

The Junior boo sah-bum nim (instructor trainee) will wear a one inch wide red, white, and blue collar stripe and will put his/her name on the back of the uniform in place of the city and state. This program is recommended for all youth in this age group.

BLACK BELT CODE OF CONDUCT:

I SHOULD ALWAYS ASK PERMISSION IF:

1.   ...I am late for class.
If a black belt is unavoidably tardy for class, he/she should bow at the edge of the workout floor and wait to be recognized by the sah-bum nim (instructor); he/she may then ask permission to join the class. (The sah-bum nim [instructor] may then assign warm-up and/or disciplinary exercises, as appropriate.)

2.   ...I <u>must</u> use the restroom during class.
Black belts should use the restroom before coming to class. If necessary, it is acceptable during class to ask permission to be excused.

3.   ...I want to workout in classes not of my specific thee (belt) level.
Receive permission from the class sah-bum nim (instructor) before each class.

4.   ...I desire to work on a poome-sae (form) or techniques of any rank higher than my own.
This is only allowed after you have tested for a new rank but have not as yet received your new rank. Never train on poome-sae (forms) or techniques higher than your current level.

5.   ...I want to instruct, correct or assist another student in Taekwondo training.
No black belt, regardless of rank, may instruct or correct another student, unless a trainee or certified sah-bum nim (instructor), without the direct, specific permission and supervision of your sah-bum nim (instructor).

6.   ...I plan to attend any non Songahm Taekwondo school or club shee-hahp (tournament).
Permission should be received before attending a non-Songahm Taekwondo school or shee-hahp (tournament) since each black belt represents the Songahm Taekwondo. While visiting another school or competition, respect should be given to sah-bum nim (Instructors) and seniors the same as you would in Songahm Taekwondo.

7.   ...I want to attempt to break boards (or other materials), practice martial arts weapons and/or desire to learn martial arts forms or techniques outside of Songahm Taekwondo.

NOTE: Permission and/or discipline will be given or withheld on an individual basis.

I SHOW MY SAH-BUM NIM (INSTRUCTORS) AND SENIORS RESPECT BY:

1.   ...standing at attention (feet together, hands by sides) and waiting to be acknowledged if I desire to converse with them.
Unless permission has been given otherwise, black belts show respect by standing at attention while addressing or being addressed by a sah-bum nim (instructor) or senior Black Belt.

2.   ...responding "Yes/No Sir", or "Yes/No Ma'am" as appropriate, in all conversations with sah-bum nim (Instructors) or higher ranked black belts.
Black belts show respect by bowing whenever greeting a sah-bum nim (instructor), in or out of the classroom. They should address sah-bum nim (Instructors) by the their surname and the proper title (Mr, Mrs, Ms, Master, etc.), regardless of any personal or family relationship.

3.   ...running to position if called by a sah-bum nim (instructor) or senior Black Belt and more than three 3 steps are required to take position in front of them.

4.   ...standing when a sah-bum nim (instructor) enters the Do-jahng, workout area, dressing rooms, or like situations.

5.   ...greeting high ranking visitors with appropriate respect and courtesy.
If class is in session, it should immediately be interrupted (by the senior student) for this situation.

6.   ...raising my hand if I do not understand a directive.
You are expected, however, to pay careful attention so the class may proceed.

7.   ...not arguing.
Questions are encouraged, argument is not. If you do not understand the answer to a question, see the sah-bum nim (instructor) after class in private and get clarification.

8.   ...turning away from my sah-bum nim (instructor) or partner when adjusting my do-bok (uniform) or thee (belt).

I SHOW RESPECT TO MY DO-JAHNG (TRAINING FACILITY) BY:

1.   ...standing during the recitation of the Songahm Spirit of Taekwondo.
If you are in the room when the "Songahm Spirit of Taekwondo" is recited, you must stand at attention and recite the pledge with the group, whether or not you are in do-bok (uniform) or a participant in the group session.

2.   ...not wearing shoes on the workout floor at any time.
If there is a physical problem that requires the use of shoes, the sah-bum nim (instructor) may give permission to wear special workout shoes.

3.   ...refraining from the use of profanity on the school premises or at any Songahm Taekwondo function, class or activity.

4.   ...being an example to other students.
Profane or rude gestures and any act that is considered to be rude or profane is not a good example for younger students.

5.   ...not making unnecessary conversation with other students and speaking only when acknowledged by or given permission by the seon-bae sah-bum nim (senior instructor) while I am participating in class.

6.   ...refraining from the use of tobacco products or alcoholic beverages while in do-bok (uniform), around a Taekwondo training facility or at <u>any Songahm Taekwondo event or function</u>.

> *NOTE: In actuality, black belts should have overcome such habits that are physically and mentally damaging to the body such as smoking, drinking, and the use of non-prescribed drugs.*

7.   ...never entering the do-jahng (Taekwondo facility) while under the influence of drugs or alcohol (see note under #5 in this section)..

8.   ...always being on time for my classes and other Taekwondo functions.

9.   ...avoiding unnecessary "playing around" in the do-jahng (Taekwondo facility), dressing rooms, waiting area or at any Taekwondo function.

The do-jahng (Taekwondo facility) is for training purposes only and black belts should be calm and in control at all times.

10.   ...telling my sah-bum nim (instructor) if I am injured.

Tell your sah-bum nim (instructor) before class. Otherwise, you will be expected to do all techniques and exercises given.

11.   ...not chewing gum while in class or working out.

12.   ...bowing in respect to the flags and training area each time I enter and/or leave the classroom area, even if the area is not being used for workout.

The correct way to bow is with your feet together, hands at your sides, bow from the waist. A bow in the Orient is about the same as a handshake in the Western world and is a sign of respect.

I CAN SHOW MY RESPECT FOR TAEKWONDO BY:

1.   ...wearing the do-bok (uniform) properly.

A Taekwondo do-bok (uniform) consists of white pants and white top, appropriate thee (belt), appropriate striping, and an organization patch which is to be worn over the right breast (the patch is presented with the orange belt). A school patch and other Songahm approved insignia are optional and should be displayed in the appropriate location with your sah-bum nim (instructor's) permission (note: some schools have special "t-shirt nights")

2.   ...treating my do-bok (uniform) and thee (belt) with respect.

Your attitude toward your do-bok (uniform) and thee (belt) reflect your attitude toward yourself and toward Taekwondo. Therefore, disrespectful treatment of you do-bok (uniform) or thee (belt) (i.e.: dragging thee [belt] on ground, wearing unkempt do-bok [uniform], etc.) is considered disrespectful.

3.   ...wearing a complete do-bok (uniform) to each class.

New students are not required to have a do-bok (uniform) immediately. Once they have a do-bok (uniform) though, they will be required to wear it to all of their classes. They must, however, have a do-bok (uniform) by the time of their first shim-sah (testing). Do-bok (uniforms) are to be worn to all shim-sah (testing).

4.   ...not rolling the pants/sleeves and always wearing full length pants/sleeves. No shorts or cutoffs permitted.

5.   ...wearing a <u>white, v-neck</u> T-shirt (or tank top) under my do-bok (uniform) (women only).

No colored T-shirts will be allowed. No T-shirts are to be worn by the men under their do-bok (uniforms), unless otherwise approved by the seon-bae sah-bum nim (senior instructor).

6.   ...always keeping my do-bok (uniform)<u>clean, pressed,</u> and <u>odor free.</u>

7.   ...wearing either my proper do-bok (uniform) or a respectful workout clothing (with sah-bum nim [instructor's] permission) during any informal workouts.
No shorts are allowed at any time.

8.   ...by never washing my Taekwondo thee (belt).
Your thee (belt) becomes soiled as you workout symbolizing all of the hard work and knowledge you have obtained.

9.   ...not wearing my thee (belt) in public.
Don't "show off" your rank. Thee (belts) should not be worn outside of the do-jahng (Taekwondo facility), except for special Taekwondo functions such as demonstrations, shee-hahp (tournaments), and award ceremonies or to and from workouts.

10.   ...keeping my hair short or restrained.
Male sah-bum nim (Instructors) are strongly encouraged to keep the hair length at or above collar length. Women with long hair should have it well restrained. Men, women, and children black belts should wear hairstyles that are considered respectable since you are always a representative of Songahm Taekwondo and have strong influence on the children and youth around you. No headbands or "sweatbands" are to be worn in class unless permission is granted by the seon-bae sah-bum nim (senior instructor).

11.   ...removing all jewelry before class.
Watches, rings, earrings, necklaces etc., WILL NOT be allowed in class or while you are in do-bok (uniform). This is for your safety and others with whom you spar. If your ring will not come off, it must be taped.

12.   ...keeping my finger and toe nails trimmed and smooth at all times.
Long, unkempt nails are not only poor grooming, but they are dangerous when you're sparring.

You are a student of Taekwondo 24 hours a day, not just while you are in the school. You are expected to conduct yourself accordingly at all times. The Songahm Spirit of Taekwondo is not just something we say in class, it is something we live by.

TO HELP KEEP GYEO-ROO-GI (SPARRING) SAFE, I MUST:

1.   ...not spar without sah-bum nim (instructor) supervision, neither in formal or informal workout sessions.

2.   ...remember that it is only practice.
Black belts will endeavor to remember that it is only practice and not try to injure their sparring partner! The sparring class is no place to develop egos. Winning and losing should not be as important as personal development and an unselfish desire to see others excel rather than beaten or humiliated by an extremely skilled martial artist..

3.   ...have my own sparring equipment.

4.   ...have and wear a mouthpiece.

5.   ...wear a groin cup (for men only).

6.   ...wear head protection during all sparring sessions.
NOTE: Students are encouraged to wear soft shin and forearm protectors.

SHEE-HAHP (TOURNAMENT) COURTESY:

1.   Black belts are allowed to change into "street clothes" at the end of their rank's competition and after all judging assignments have been completed.
They are then free to leave the premises or enjoy the shee-hahp (tournament) as a spectator.

2.   Encourage students and spectators to stay in spectator areas, leaving ring areas clear for current competitors.
You can do this not only by directive but also by example.

3.   Regulation do-bok (uniforms) and thee (belts) are required.
White tennis shoes may be worn while in do-bok (uniform) when the black belt is not competing. The do-bok (uniform) may be lettered, according to organization regulations, to identify the competitor's home school.

4.   Black belts will bow to the flags each time they enter or leave the shee-hahp (tournament) room.

5.   Fellow competitors are first fellow Songahm students.
The competitive spirit must not preclude courtesy and respect. Black belts are encouraged to support friends in an enthusiastic, friendly, positive manner. No negative or derisive comments are tolerated.

6.   Black belts will answer enthusiastically; they will bow before entering the ring and bow and thank the judges upon being dismissed from the ring.

7.   Black belts will address their opponents in a courteous manner, wishing them well before the match begins and thanking them when the match is completed.

8.   Black belts, whether or not in do-bok (uniform), will display respect and courtesy to all other students, sah-bum nim (Instructors), and guests.
There is often limited seating at shee-hahp (tournaments). Guests should be offered available chairs.

9.   Every Songahm Taekwondo student, whether or not in do-bok (uniform) and whether or not a competitor, will stand at attention and recite the "Songahm Spirit of Taekwondo" with the participants.

10.   Each black belt will conduct themselves in a manner that brings honor to themselves, their school, and their organization.
Many spectators are new to the martial arts and may form opinions based on the actions and attitudes of students.

SHIM-SAH (TESTING) COURTESIES:

1.   Black belts should arrive in plenty of time to warm up. *Because the workout area is more crowded than usual with students and spectators, group warm-up is limited.*

2.   Black belts must be dressed in a clean, regulation do-bok (uniform) with the correct thee (belt).

3.   Spectators are welcome at shim-sah (testing), but they must be quiet and non-interruptive during the proceedings; because the shim-sah (testing) is often long, sah-bum nim (Instructors) discourage the attendance of babies and small children.

4.   Courtesy to other students includes being quiet and attentive as fellow students test. Enthusiastic, positive encouragement is permitted during the gyeo-roo-gi (sparring) portion of the shim-sah (testing).

5.   A black belt who is scheduled to test, but finds himself unable to attend, should notify the sah-bum nim (instructor) before the shim-sah (testing) begins.

6.   Black belts who are testing will remain with the group until shim-sah (testing) is complete.

7.   Black belts who are attending the shim-sah (testing) as spectators will stand at attention and recite the Songahm Spirit of Taekwondo, whether or not in do-bok (uniform).

GENERAL GUIDELINES:

1.   Rank is an Honor, but more it is a RESPONSIBILITY!
It is the responsibility of sah-bum nim (Instructors), Black Belts and Senior students to assist the lower ranks in learning the art and disciplines of Taekwondo. All lower ranks are encouraged to respectfully ask for assistance and individual help from any of their seniors.

2.   Parents and guests are bound by the same rules of conduct while they are in or around the do-jahng (Taekwondo facility) or at a Taekwondo function, wherever it may be.

3.   Treat every other student with the respect and courtesy that you as a student want and expect to receive.
Remember, the key to all relationships between people is mutual respect and courtesy.

4.   The Senior black belt among black belts of the same rank is the one who achieved the rank first.
If the rank was earned at the same time, seniority may be determined by length in Taekwondo or by age. A sah-bum nim (instructor) may also prefer to rotate the senior position.

5.   Students, parents, and guests will not converse with any person involved in a class session without permission of the sah-bum nim (instructor).

6.   Complaints, infractions or violations of the moral and/ or ethical standards of Songahm Taekwondo should be reported in the proper order: Student, to sah-bum nim (instructor), to seon-bae sah-bum nim (senior instructor), to Regional Vice President to National Officer, to President. All complaints and opinions dealing with the school or sah-bum nim (Instructors) will be brought to the attention of the seon-bae sah-bum nim (senior instructor) and NOT into dressing room conversation.

7.   If a student is suspended, their presence is suspended from all Songahm Taekwondo schools and functions for the period of their suspension.

8.   Clothing worn around the students must be of good condition (no holes, bleached, ragged, etc.) and must set an example of the quality of their school.

9.   When attending any event, black belts must wear either a Songahm Taekwondo instructor's suit, do-bok (uniform), suit and tie (or ladies equivalent) or approved staff outfit.
If at a Songahm Taekwondo event, only the instructor's suit, suit and tie or do-bok (uniform) is permitted.

10.   Black belts must abide by the student rules regarding appearance at all times as an example to students (fingernail length, jewelry, etc.)

11.   Songahm Taekwondo requires that black belts must have passed their time requirement, attended an average of two classes per week, and received their sah-bum nim (instructor's) permission to test.

12.   Certified\trainee sah-bum nim (Instructors): Failure to maintain average weekly classes and\or sah-bum nim (instructor) requirements, may result in disciplinary action (i.e.: probation, removal from trainee program, removal from club operation, etc.)

13.   Black belts must inform the seon-bae sah-bum nim (senior instructor), personally, if he\she will not be attending black belt class.

14.   Black belts scheduled to teach or assist in a class must make arrangements with the class sah-bum nim (instructor) or seon-bae sah-bum nim (senior instructor) to have a replacement.

15.   Improper conduct as a class sah-bum nim (instructor) or assistant is not tolerated.

16.   Black belts must attend all school and Songahm Taekwondo events unless permission has been granted to miss the event.

17.   Alcoholic consumption is not permitted when you are a representative of your school. This includes any time a Songahm Taekwondo student (especially a minor) is present.

18.   The use of, sale of or association with any non-prescribed drug or prescribed drug abuse will not be tolerated.

19.   Black belts will be an example of the Spirit of Taekwondo in their daily lives and will uphold and enforce the rules and regulations of the Songahm Taekwondo and student\black belt manuals.

20.   "Passing the buck" is not acceptable.
If you are directly asked by your senior to perform a duty, you are to perform that duty. Do not "pass" that duty to a lower rank.

21.   Understand that if handled improperly, a student\black belt relationship with members of the opposite sex could be devastating for a student's or black belt's Taekwondo training.
Since Taekwondo is the number one concern, a relationship with a student

or family member of a student should be sincere and handled with care. A failure in the relationship could result in failure of one or both parties continuing their Taekwondo training. Don't use your position to force relationships. It is not permitted for Songahm Taekwondo black belts and sah-bum nim (Instructors) to date men or women that are married. It is forbidden for adult (18 and over) black belts and sah-bum nim (Instructors) to have relationships with minors.

22.   Black belts (especially trainee or certified,) should not socialize in a personal manner with students unless he\she feels this personal time is to the benefit of the student.

23.   Quite often, students will do "anything" for their sah-bum nim (instructor) or anyone representing their sah-bum nim (instructor). This is the basis for proper training. By abusing this, the sah-bum nim (instructor) or black belt limits his\her ability to teach that student.

Many times the student will offer to help a black belt due to the sense of loyalty that student has to "do" for you. Rather, let that student ask what he can do for you. Do not allow a student to abuse himself for your benefit... make sure that student receives something in return for their services.

24.   Black belts (student status) may assist classes periodically but must be certified or on the sah-bum nim (instructor) training program to be allowed to assist on a regular basis.

Black belts are asked to keep the spirit of these rules and not just the words.

MASTER
CESAR
OZUNA

6th Degree
Tae-sah Nim

MASTER
TAMMY
HARVEY
LAMBERSON

6th Degree
Tae-sah Nim

연 습

CHAPTER IX: TRAINING

In this chapter on training, we will cover two very different aspects of your Taekwondo training. The first is called *advanced stretching* and the second part is about training in the *weapons of Songahm Taekwondo.*

It is important to understand that both activities covered in this chapter have the potential of serious injury if not practiced correctly and under the direct supervision of a certified sah-bum nim (Instructor). Please do not think that because you have achieved the rank of cho dan (1st degree) that it somehow qualifies you as an expert on stretching or weapons. Seek proper approval from your sah-bum nim (instructor) before pursuing the use of any weapon or before trying any exercise in this chapter.

WARNING: Songahm Taekwondo suggests that you receive a proper check-up and discuss any new exercises you begin with your physician before attempting them. Songahm Taekwondo and its affiliates are not responsible for any injuries sustained by the practice of any of the following exercises.

ACTIVE/PASSIVE (A/P) STRETCHING:

The following exercises are designed to take black belts beyond the point at which they feel like they have "leveled out" in their ability to stretch. This should enhance, not replace, a regular stretching routine.

It is very important that you follow every directive concering each exercise. You and your partner should take this stretching program very seriously, as unlike most other stretching routines, this has a greater risk factor involved because you are depending on your partner to know what you are feeling.

What is "active/passive" stretching?

This type of stretching is actually very good for your muscles and safer than regular stretching when the rules are followed correctly. Read the following rules that apply to all three of the exercises.

The person who is actually stretching (referred to hereafter as "you") plays a passive role until the moment at which he/she will begin actively stretching. The partner (referred to hereafter as "your partner") is most responsible for your safety. This is because you are to totally relax and allow your partner to prepare you for each stretch session (a stretch session is a 10 second interval during which you apply pressure to your partner's resistance).

Stretching Rules

1. Your partner is to <u>always move slowly.</u> Under no circumstances are any of these exercises to bounce, move quickly, or be pushed past the relaxed stretching point while relaxed.

2. Your partner should be sure to have solid support and never depend on you or any part of your body for that support.

3. Your partner is not the one who should determine "how far" you can stretch. This is up to you and your partner should follow your instructions <u>without question</u>.

4. All exercises should be done in 10 second stretch sessions with 5 second intervals between each.

The Proceedure

1. You assume the pre-stretch position.
2. Your partner should then assume his/her pre-stretch position.
3. Your partner should press the legs toward the desired goal until they have reached maximum relaxed stretch position.
4. Your partner should tighten his/her muscles (not applying additional pressure to your muscles) so as to make your legs immoveable.
5. You apply pressure against your partner's resistance for a count of ten.
6. Relax for five seconds during which time your partner presses your legs slowly to a new relaxed stretch position now made avaiable as a result of your ten second session.
7. Repeat numbers 4 through 6 two more times for a total of three stretch sessions. Then go to number 8.
8. Finally, allow your partner to slowly return your legs to a comfortable position. Stand up slowly as your legs should be exhausted by now.

NOTE: Repeat this training exercise every two days or more. Do not apply the same type of exercise to the same muscles within a 36 to 48 hour period.

A/P BUTTERFLY

You: Lie on the floor with the bottoms of your feet together. Try to pull the heels of your feet as close to your body as possible. Allow your knees to relax downward to the floor.

Your Partner: Your partner should place his/her feet together just below yours. Then, slowly place his/her knees on top of yours. Follow the procedure suggested at the beginning of this chapter while pressing your knees toward the floor. Your partner should hold your thee (belt) for more

control as you are to apply pressure upward with maximum strength during your 10 second stretch session.

After using this active/passive (A/P) stretching for a period of time, you may be able to stretch as Master G. K. Lee demonstrates (photo, left).

A/P FRONT SPLITS

You: Assume a position lying on your back with one leg in the air (repeat this exercise with both legs). You must attempt to keep both hips level with the floor and both knees straight.

Your partner: Places one foot on your dobok (uniform) pants near the knee of the leg that is on the ground. This is to help keep your leg down and your knee straight. Placing your other foot over his/her collarbone, your partner should grab your lapel for support. Your partner should then lean forward until your leg is at the maximum relaxed stretch. Following the procedure at the beginning of this chapter, your partner should hold his/her position while you apply maximum force against him/her as if you were trying to force your leg back down to the ground.

After you have completed three times with this exercise, your partner should bend your knee and force your knee toward your chest while allowing the foot to rest near the buttocks. Then, your partner should stretch your leg back out and lay it on the ground.

Repeat this proceedure with the opposite leg.

A/P SIDE SPLITS

This is the third and probably most serious of the three stretches. Take care to move very slowly and your partner should not attempt to push you beyond your maximum relaxed stretch.

You: Lay on the floor with your buttocks against a wall (in this case Master G. K. Lee is against a mirror). Lift your legs straight up the wall and then allow them to relax to each side.

Your Partner: Places his/her left leg in front of your right leg. His/her right leg is softly placed on the knee of your left leg. Your partner then holds your right leg with his/her left arm. Now, he/she slowly presses toward the floor until you have reached your maximum relaxed stretch position. While following the procedure at the beginning of this chapter, attempt to pull your legs straight up as if to put your ankles together.

When you have completed three 10 second stretch sessions, have your partner slowly lift your legs up toward each other to a comfortable position.

Use these three exercises diligently and on a regular schedule and you will see results nearly right away. Many students have seen substantial results in two or three sessions. However, don't worry if it takes your muscles a little longer. Everybody's body is different and if yours chooses to take longer to change in some areas, let it....it knows what is best for your body type.

SONGAHM TAEKWONDO WEAPONS:

Songahm Taekwondo expands beyond the basic art with the PROTECH TRAINING SYSTEMS' seminars for black belts and sah-bum nim (instructors).

Protech offers a variety of training. The following are courses that can be attended by Songahm black belts and Sah-bum nim (instructors): Pressure Point Control Tactics, Spontaneous Knife Defense, Joint Manipulation & Throwing Techniques, Single/Double Stick & Disarming, Sexual Harassment Assault & Rape Prevention, Defense Tactics Course, Ssahng Jeol Bong, and Jahng Bong. If you are interested in attending any of the classes offered, see your sah-bum nim (instructor) for details.

JAHNG BONG (Long Staff)

Pictured above is the Jahng Bong or long staff. This weapon is one of the most effective long range weapons used in early Korea. It is a combination of Chinese, Korean, and Japanese techniques, taking the best from each style. The benefits include increased self defense skills and tremendous upper body strength, as well as improved concentration, coordination, focus and self-confidence.

BONG MAHNG-EE
(Single & Double Stick)

This course is great for the development of "hand - eye" coordination. This course gives the student basics for training in just about any weapons system.

Developed from a stick used to beat the water out of clothes (a method of drying and pressing), the stick found its use as a weapon when the young ladies would have to defend themselves against attackers while alone at home, doing the laundry. The history behind this Korean weapon lends a sense of enchantment to the destructive force it can bring.

SPONTANEOUS KNIFE DEFENSE

Songahm's Protech division offers extensive training in Spontaneous Knife Defense and weapons disarming. It focuses on the Filipino knife system and offers an inside look at how knives are used in combat and how to defend against the knife, one of the most dangerous weapons used today in the streets.

SSAHNG JEOL BONG (Nunchucku)

A must on every "karate kid's" list is to learn how to do the Ssahng Jeol Bong (Korean for nunchucku). This course is offered, however, to adult high ranking black belts and is great to develop tremendous upper body strength and improved concentration, coordination, focus and self-confidence.

MASTER
MIKE
CARUSO

6th Degree
Tae-sah Nim

MASTER
MICHAEL
HEMANN

6th Degree
Tae-sah Nim

기타 APPENDIX

A: ADVANCED BODY TARGETS (Front)

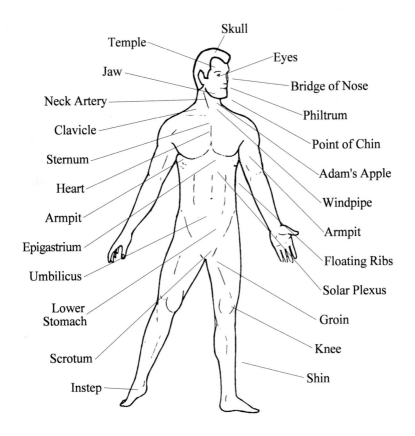

B: ADVANCED BODY TARGETS (Back)

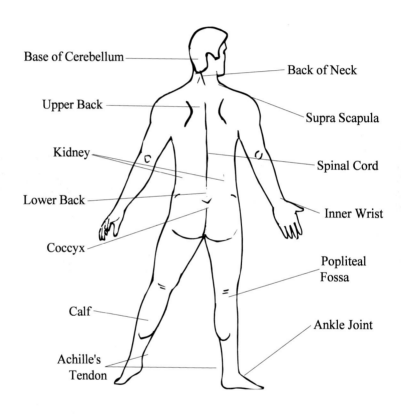

Base of Cerebellum

Back of Neck

Upper Back

Supra Scapula

Kidney

Spinal Cord

Lower Back

Inner Wrist

Coccyx

Popliteal Fossa

Calf

Ankle Joint

Achille's Tendon

C: PRESSURE POINTS

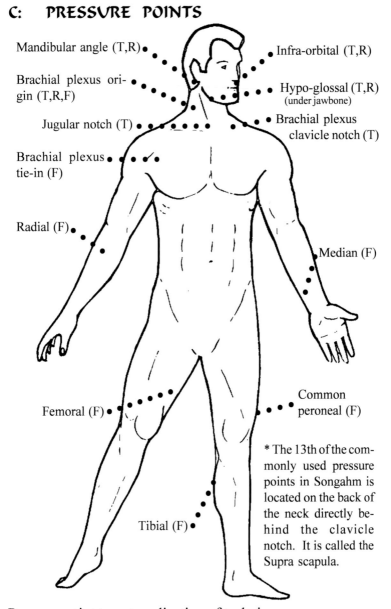

Mandibular angle (T,R)

Infra-orbital (T,R)

Brachial plexus origin (T,R,F)

Hypo-glossal (T,R)
(under jawbone)

Jugular notch (T)

Brachial plexus clavicle notch (T)

Brachial plexus tie-in (F)

Radial (F)

Median (F)

Femoral (F)

Common peroneal (F)

* The 13th of the commonly used pressure points in Songahm is located on the back of the neck directly behind the clavicle notch. It is called the Supra scapula.

Tibial (F)

Pressure point target application of technique:

T = Apply touch pressure
R = Apply raking action
F = Apply fluid shock wave

D: ENGLISH/KOREAN TRANSLATION

eo = is the same as the <u>u</u> sound "suffer"

eh = is the same sound as the <u>ea</u> in "death"

o = the long <u>o</u> as in "go"

g = g as in "good"

oo = as sounded in "zoo"

y = always used as its sound in "yell"

ee/i = as the <u>ee</u> in "see"

ah = as in "father"

eu = the <u>oo</u> as in "good"

    The above sounds are displayed below in *italics*.

- **r** = to "roll" the <u>r</u> as used in Spanish
- **Bold** print shows sounds that belong together (example: say "y*eo*ng," now add a "k" sound to the beginning; **k** + **y***eo*ng = **ky***eo*ng as in the word for <u>attention</u>, **ky***eo*ng-n*eh*).
- A double letter (example: Ss or Bb) reminds you to emphasize the sound.

POSITIONS (Jah-sae)

Attention Position	M*o-ah* J*ah*-s*ae*
Half-command Position	B*ah*n J*ee*-d*o* -j*ah* J*ah*-s*ae*
Natural Ready Position	J*ah*-y*eo*n J*ah*-s*ae*
Sparring Position	**Gy***eo*-**r***oo*-g*i* J*ah*-s*ae*

STANCES (Seo-gi)

Attention Stance	M*o-ah* S*eo*-g*i*
Back Stance	Duw*ee*t-goo-b*ee* S*eo*-g*i*
Closed Stance	M*o-ah* S*eo*-g*i*
Front Stance	*Ah*p-goo-b*ee* S*eo*-g*i*
Low Closed Stance	Goob-*eu*n M*o-ah* S*eo*-g*i*
Middle Stance	J*oo*-ch*oo*m S*eo*-g*i*
Parallel Stance	N*ah*-**r***ah*n-h*ee* S*eo*-g*i*
Rear Stance	B*eo*m S*eo*-g*i*
Sparring Stance	**Gy***eo*-**r***oo*-g*i* S*eo*-g*i*

BLOCKS & STRIKES
Blocks (Mahk-gi)

9-Block	K*oo*-j*ah* M*ah*k-g*i*
Front 9-Block	*Ah*p K*oo*-j*ah* M*ah*k-g*i*
Half-low Block	B*ah*n *Ah*-**r***ae* M*ah*k-g*i*
High Block	U*i* M*ah*k-g*i*
High/Low Block	U*i*/*Ah*-**r***ae* M*ah*k-g*i*
Inner-forearm Block	*Ah*n P*ah*l-mok M*ah*k-g*i*

Knifehand Block	Sohn-nahl Mahk-gi
Knifehand High Block	Sohn-nahl Ui Mahk-gi
Knifehand Low Block	Sohn-nahl Ah-rae Mahk-gi
Low Block	Ah-rae Mahk-gi
Outer-forearm Block	Bah-kaht Pahl-mok Mahk-gi
Ridgehand Strike	Eop-eun Sohn-nahl Mahk-gi
Square Block	Sah-gahk Mahk-gi
X-Block	Eot-geol

Strikes (Chi-gi)

Backfist Strike	Deung Ju-meok Chi-gi
Elbow Strike	Pahl-goop Chi-gi
Fingertip Thrust	Sohn-geut Jee-reu-gi
Head Grab	Mok-teol-mee Jahp-kee
Knifehand Strike	Sohn-nahl Chi-gi
Palm Strike	Bah-tahng Sohn Chi-gi
Punch	Jee-reu-gi
Vertical Fingertip Thrust	Sae-woon Sohn-geut Jee-reu-gi

KICKS (Chah-gi)

(the th in this word is pronounced with a hard release)

Foot Stomp	Jee Keo
Front Kick	Ahp Chah-gi
Hook Kick	Nahk-ah Chah-gi
Jump Front Kick	Ddee-eo Ahp Chah-gi
Knee Strike	Moo-reup Chi-gi
Pressing Side Kick	Mee-reo Yeop Chah-gi
Round Kick	Dol-ryeo Chah-gi
Stretch Kick	Ahp Ol-reo Chah-gi
Side Kick	Yeop Chah-gi

TECHNICAL ENHANCEMENTS

Double	Doo
Compound	Jong-hahp
Circular	Weon
Horizontal	Soo-pyeong
Inward	Ahn Johk
Jump	Ddee-eo
Reverse	Bahn-dae
Spin	Dol-ah
Twin	Ssahng
Upset	Jae-chyeo
Vertical	Sae-woon

OTHER

Attention	Ch*ah*-r*e*ot
At ease	Sh*i*-uh
Belt	Th*ee*
Bow	**Ky**eong-neh
Break (in sparring)	K*ah*lee-*eo*h
Degree (rank)	Dan (D*ah*n)
End	B*ah*-ro
Form	Poome-sae
Fist	Joo-me*o*k
Grade (rank)	Ge*u*p
Instructor	S*ah*-bum nim (S*ah*-be*o*m n*i*m)
1-step sparring	Il-bo **gy**eo-r*oo*-g*i*
Ready	June-b*ee*
Self-defense	Ho-sh*i*n-s*oo*l
Sparring	**Gy**eo-r*oo*-gi
Start	She-j*ah*k
Stop	K*eu*-m*ah*n
Taekwondo facility	D*o*-j*ah*ng
Testing	Shim-sah
Uniform	D*o*-bok
Yell	K*i*-h*a*p

NUMBERS

English	*Korean*	*Old Korean*	*Numbering*
1 one	h*ah*-n*ah*	*i*l	Il-jahng, Il-beon
2 two	d*oo*l	*ee*	Ee-jahng, Ee-beon
3 three	set	s*ah*m	Sahm-jahng, Sahm-beon
4 four	net	s*ah*	Sah-jahng, Sah-beon
5 five	d*ah*-seot	oh	
6 six	y*e*o-seot	y*oo*k	
7 seven	*i*l-ge*u*p	ch*i*l	
8 eight	y*e*o-d*o*l	p*ah*l	
9 nine	*ah*-hop	k*oo*	
10 ten	y*e*ol	ship	
20 twenty	s*oo*-mool	*ee*-ship	
30 thirty	s*e*o-r*eu*n	s*ah*m-ship	
40 forty	m*ah*-he*u*n	s*ah*-ship	
50 fifty	shw*ee*-he*u*n	oh-ship	
60 sixty	yea-se*u*n	y*oo*k-ship	
70 seventy	*ee*-r*eu*n	ch*i*l-ship	
80 eighty	y*e*o-d*eu*n	p*ah*l-ship	
90 ninety	*ah*-he*u*n	k*oo*-ship	
100 hundred	beck	baek	

E: KOREAN TERMINOLOGY

Ah-he*u*n	Ninety (90)
Ah-h*o*p	Nine (9)
*Ah*n J*o*hk	Inward
*Ah*n P*a*hl-m*o*k M*a*hk-*gi*	Inner-forearm Block
*Ah*p Ch*ah*-*gi*	Front Kick
*Ah*p-g*oo*-bee S*eo*-*gi*	Front Stance
Ahp-koo-jah Mahk-gi	Front 9-block
*Ah*p *O*l-r*eo* Ch*ah*-*gi*	Stretch Kick
Ah-**r**ae M*a*hk-*gi*	Low Block
B*ah*-k*a*ht P*a*hl-m*o*k M*a*hk-*gi*	Outer-forearm Block
B*ah*n *Ah*-rae M*a*hk-*gi*	Half-low Block
B*ah*n-*jee*-d*o*-j*ah* J*a*h-s*ae*	Half-command Position
B*ah*n-dae	Reverse
B*ah*-**r**o	End
B*ah*-t*ah*ng S*o*hn	Palm
Baek	One-hundred (100)
B*eo*m S*eo*-*gi*	Rear Stance
B*oo* S*a*h-*bum* n*i*m	Trainee Instructor
Chah-gi	Kick
Ch*ah*-**r**e*o*t	Attention
Chi-gi	Strike
Ch*i*l	Seven (7)
Ch*i*l-ship	Seventy (70)
Ch*o*-dan (Ch*o*-d*ah*n)	1st degree (beginner)
Ch*o*-dan (Ch*o*-d*ah*n) Y*ae*-bee	1st degree recommended
Dan (D*ah*n)	Degree (rank)
D*ah*-se*o*t	Five (5)
Dd*ee*-*eo*	Jump
De*u*ng	Back
De*u*ng J*oo*-me*o*k Ch*i*-*gi*	Backfist Strike
D*o*-b*o*k	Uniform
D*o*-j*ah*ng	Taekwondo Facility
Dol-ah	Spin
D*o*l-**ry***eo* Ch*ah*-*gi*	Round Kick
D*oo*-bah-kaht Pahl-mok Mahk-*gi*	Double Outer-forearm Block
D*oo*-sohn-n*ah*l M*a*hk-*gi*	Double Knifehand Block
D*oo*l	Two (2)
Duw*ee*t-*goo*-*bee* Seo-gi	Back Stance
Ee	Two (2)
Ee-ship	Twenty (20)
Ee-**r**e*u*n	Seventy (70)
*Eo*p-*eu*n S*o*hn-n*ah*l	Ridgehand
*Eo*t-ge*o*l	X-block
Ui M*a*hk-*gi*	High block

Gae-*in* chi-do	Private Lesson
Gae Gae-*in*	Private (one-on-one)
Ge*u*p	Grade (rank)
Goob-*eu*n	Sparring
Gyeo-ʀoo-gi Boo-boon	Sparring Segments
Gyeo-ʀoo-gi Jah-sae	Sparring Position
Gyeo-ʀoo-gi Seo-gi	Sparring Stance
H*ah*-n*ah*	One (1)
Ho-shin-sool	Self-defense
Il	One (1)
Il-b*o* **gy**eo-ʀoo-gi	1-step sparring
Il-ge*u*p	Seven (7)
Jae-chyeo	Upset
Jee Keo	Foot Stomp
J*ah*-yeon J*ah*-sae	Natural Ready Position
J*ah*-sae	Position
Jee-ʀeu-gi	Punch
Jong-h*ah*p	Compound
Joo-choom Seo-gi	Middle Stance
Joo-me*o*k	Fist
June-b*ee*	Ready
K*ah*l-ry*eo*	Break (in sparring)
Ke*u*-m*ah*n	Stop
Koo	Nine (9)
Koo-j*ah* M*ah*k-gi	9-block
Koo-ship	Ninety (90)
K*i*-h*a*p	Yell
Kyeong-neh	Bow
M*ah*-he*u*n	Forty (40)
M*ah*k-gi	Blocks
Mee-ʀeo Yeop Ch*ah*-gi	Pressing Side Kick
Mo-ah Seo-gi	Attention Stance
Mok-teol-mee Jahp-kee	Head Grab
Moo-ʀeup Ch*i*-gi	Knee Strike
N*ah*k-*ah* Ch*ah*-gi	Hook Kick
N*ah*-ʀahn-hee Seo-gi	Parallel Stance
Net	Four (4)
Oh	Five (5)
Oh-ship	Fifty (50)
P*ah*l	Eight (8)
P*ah*l-goop Ch*i*-gi	Elbow Strike
P*ah*l-ship	Eighty (80)
Poome-sae	Form
Pil-yo Sah-hahng	Requirements
Sae-woon	Vertical

Sah	Four (4)
Sah-gahk Mahk-gi	Square Block
Sah-bum nim (Sah-beom nim)	Instructor
Sah-ship	Forty (40)
Sahm	Three (3)
Sahm-ship	Thirty (30)
Seon-bae Sah-bum nim	Senior Instructor
Seo-reun	Thirty (30)
Seo-gi	Stance
Set	Three (3)
She-hahp	Tournament
She-jahk	Start
Shim-sah	Testing
Ship	Ten (10)
Shi-uh	At Ease
Shwee-heun	Fifty (50)
Soo-mool	Twenty (20)
Sohn-geut Jee-reu-gi	Fingertip Thrust
Sohn-nahl Chi-gi	Knifehand Strike
Sohn-nahl Ah-rae Mahk-gi	Knifehand Low Block
Sohn-nahl Ui Mahk-gi	Knifehand High Block
Soo-pyeong	Horizontal
Ssahng	Twin
Ssahng Ah-rae Mahk-gi	Twin Low Block
Thee	Belt
Ui Mahk-gi	High Block
Ui/ah-rae Mahk-gi	High/low Block
Weon	Circular
Yae-bee	Recommended (rank)
Yea-seun	Sixty (60)
Yeo-dol	Eight (8)
Yeo-deun	Eighty (80)
Yeol	Ten (10)
Yeop Chah-gi	Side Kick
Yeo-seot	Six (6)
Yook	Six (6)

F: STVDENT HISTORY

This book belongs to _____

Date received Black Belt _____ Age _____

Height _____ Weight _____ School Grade _____

Black Belt classmates _____
_____
_____

Other Taekwondo friends _____
_____

Date I want to test for 2nd degree _____

Date I want to test for Trainee _____

My interests outside of Taekwondo _____

Before my next testing, I would like to improve this in my life
_____

My philosophy of Life _____

My Life's goal (one sentence) _____
_____

My Chief Instructor _____ Rank _____

My Class Instructor _____ Rank _____

My Taekwondo School _____

When I look back at the days when I was just a color belt, I wish that I had made records of my progress. I have no written records or photographs of my early Taekwondo history. Only my memory. I highly recommend that you fill this out completely.

Grand Master Lee

G: AUTHOR

GRAND MASTER H. U. LEE
Songahm Founder and Sah-boo nim

Sahboo Nim, Grand Master Haeng Ung Lee, is the Founder of the American Taekwondo Association, Songahm Taekwondo Federation, and World Traditional Taekwondo Union.

Although he is the world's leading innovator of martial arts, he holds to a traditional standard that most arts have lost. His great endeavor to create a comprehensive encyclopedia of Taekwondo has logged thousands of man hours. However, he has produced the most authoritative training manuals ever developed on any single martial art.

His knowledge and skill as a Taekwondo master and his sincere outreach to the young and old for the purpose of helping them become who they want to be, is the epitome of the martial artist.

H: ACKNOWLEDGMENTS

Many sah-bum nim (Instructors), students, and others with concerns about the growth of Songahm Taekwondo have made contributions over the decades to Grand Master Lee and Traditional Taekwondo. The following list in no way can express the gratitude we have for the unselfish devotion of the innovators of the past. Therefore, this list reflects the people who gave of their time, effort, creativity, and knowledge to bring about the production of such a vital part of Songahm Taekwondo.

TRANSCRIBING AND EDITING:
Mr. Ron Lewis

ASSISTANT EDITORS:
Master Mal Kun Lee, Instruction consistency
Miss Faith Stuart, General editing
Mr. Jay Kohl, General editing
Ms. Sherri Williams

GRAPHICS AND DESIGN
Mr. Ron Lewis, Layout and design
Miss Faith Stuart, Graphics assistant

SONGAHM FORMS DEVELOPMENT COMMITTEE:
Grand Master Haeng Ung Lee, Chairman
Master Bill Clark, Vice Chairman
Senior Master Robert Allemier
Senior Master In Ho Lee

MODELS:
Master Soon Ho Lee
Master Gyung Kun "G. K." Lee
Mr. Taekwon Lee

DIGITAL PHOTOGRAPHY:
Mr. Ron Lewis

SPECIAL NOTES